INFLATION:
Everyone's Problem

By Arthur Milton

Life Insurance Stocks: The Modern Gold Rush
How to Get a Dollar's Value for a Dollar Spent
Something More Can Be Done!
Life Insurance Stocks: An Investment Appraisal

Arthur Milton

INFLATION:
Everyone's Problem

THE CITADEL PRESS
NEW YORK

42032

Dedication:

To AMERICA'S YOUTH . . . . Not to the few whose antics
fill the headlines, but to the millions of alert, eager and
idealistic young men and women who carry on the
destinies of this great nation, I dedicate this book.

It is they who finally must solve the problem of inflation;
it is they who must hold aloft the lamp of freedom;
and it is to them that we pass along both the precious
benefits and sober obligations of free-enterprise society.

And yet, in passing, we should remember the "little"
people—those who toiled honestly to help make freedom
and free enterprise a vibrant thing. One such person was
my father, Herman, who by unfortunate coincidence
died on the very day this book was completed.

First Edition
Copyright © 1968 by Arthur Milton. All rights reserved. Published
by Citadel Press, Inc., 222 Park Avenue South, New York, N.Y.
10003. Published simultaneously in Canada by George J. McLeod
Limited, 73 Bathurst Street, Toronto 2B, Ontario.
Manufactured in the United States of America by
The Haddon Craftsmen, Inc., Scranton, Pa.
Library of Congress Catalog Card Number: 68-28445.

PREFACE

RUNAWAY INFLATION IS a powerful destroyer of opportunity. Even creeping inflation, which is more or less continuous in human history, can frighten people enough to weaken their incentive and their resolve to work hard and be thrifty.

In spite of the great unrest in the world, and in our own country in particular, I am firmly convinced that the future never has been brighter, if we will just take reasonable precautions against runaway inflation. There are so many opportunities for Americans today that the sky really is the limit. Young America again is on the march. The hippy movement is on the wane, and within a year should be only a memory like the flapper era right after World War I. Every generation of young Americans has had its share of rebels. My own generation was looked on with considerable dismay (and some self-pitying sentimentality) as "the lost generation," but not too many of us stayed lost. Sooner or later, like the youngsters of the present generation, most of us were bright enough to realize that America remains the land of opportunity and will remain so for many generations.

Right now there is a tremendous demand in this country for more food and more goods and services. New industries are springing up to satisfy these demands and everyone who is willing to apply himself and work hard has opportunities today that his parents would not have dreamed possible.

The population of the United States recently passed 200 million and in another ten years will top 240 million. There is every indication that our Gross National Product will reach one trillion dollars by the mid-1970s. And what will make all this possible is the American free enterprise system. It is the difference between this system and all the other governmental systems in the world that has enabled the people of our country to take advantage of its vast resources so efficiently.

We must remember that our system extends much latitude for many attitudes. It is that fact—our freedom of choice to be self-employed—our right to seek out one employer instead of another—our right to purchase what we will in the free market—our right to choose to spend and invest our money wherever we please—that has been the American way and it will continue to be so.

The origins of this system go back to pre-Revolutionary days. Since 1776, the basic principles underlying our government have not been changed and they will continue to prevail.

Our freedom of choice and our great tolerance for varying attitudes permit us to embrace collective social action for the common good without making it a matter of slavish dogma. Our programs to relieve poverty and build a Great Society reflect this fact. Such collective action usually is accompanied by giveaways and gimmicks which most of us accept or tolerate as part of the price man must pay for being a political animal.

But I, for one, remain firmly convinced that no one has a right to what another has earned. To claim that some people enjoy such a right is to encourage theft, corruption and insurrection. There must be a grass-roots effort once again to lift the sights of our population and persuade those on relief and those whom the poverty program is designed to help to regain their self-respect by working.

Politicians are mostly to blame for the giveaways and gimmicks; they find it politically expedient to encourage trends that could unwittingly lead to corruption and then to socialism or communism. And unfortunately, there are many people who are willing to go along with these ideas while knowing they are wrong.

To bring the matter down to the specific points of this book, far too many of us are lazy in our thinking, or too willing to drift along with trends in our economic policy that, by leading us into runaway inflation, could destroy most of the bright opportunities ahead of us.

Let's stop being so foolish.

A.M.

New York

CONTENTS

INTRODUCTION

IT IS THE intention of this book to show that, while inflation is the means by which society pays for social and economic progress, and therefore over the long pull is inevitable, consumers can always halt inflation anytime it becomes perilous. All they need is the will to do so.

If we all drove our automobiles without rhyme or reason and without the aid of traffic lights and rules of the road, unimaginable chaos and disaster would quickly result. Yet there are people now living who can remember when you didn't even have to register an automobile; drivers' licenses didn't come into general use until the 1930s. The stop-and-go traffic light wasn't invented until the mid-1920s, when automobiles had already been in use more than thirty years. It wasn't until the end of World War II that the majority of motorists carried liability insurance.

We can stop the car whenever we come to a red light, whenever we feel too tired to drive farther, or whenever we feel we are spending too much money on gas and tires. Yet the purpose of owning an automobile is to be able to keep on the move—hopefully, to keep progressing toward the personal goals of prosperity and the pursuit of happiness.

The automobile has also been an inflationary influence. First the desire, then, as the pace of social change accelerated, the need to have a car caused young people to go into debt much earlier in life than would have been considered either wise or ethical by past generations. Yet our society learned to cope with this too—to call periodic halts on the inflation caused by the automobile by putting off for a year or so the purchase of new cars. So, I am convinced, it is or should be with all inflation. We have the power to stop any inflationary spiral dead in its tracks whenever it threatens to go off on a runaway course.

To do this we don't need the leadership of the politicians and the powers that rule the business community. On the contrary, we can command them to do our bidding. We can rule the politicians by the exercise of our ballots. As for the businessmen, we can hold a much tighter rein on them if we will, controlling them by simply withholding purchasing power.

That brings us to the most important point of all—ourselves. In order to exercise our power to make inflation grind to a halt, we must exercise personal self-control. First of all, we must understand the real nature of inflation, the different types of inflation, and the historical development of inflation. Then we will know, as individual consumers, how and when we should step firmly on the brakes.

ARTHUR MILTON

INFLATION:
Everyone's Problem

1.

INFLATION
IS ETERNAL

For the first time in about a century, Americans have recently felt the impact of palpable inflation. We have not experienced any real harm from the inflation and we probably won't. But many Americans are worried about it.

They have read how galloping inflation has ravaged so many peoples, even strong nations, in our time in Europe, Latin America, Asia and Africa. The economics, and hence the political and social climates, of some of these countries are prostrate from inflation even as this is being written.

Some millions of Americans had to live through galloping inflation in the lands of their birth before they came to our shores—or their parents did. They know at firsthand, or from what their parents have told them, how uncontrolled inflation crushes and stultifies the human spirit, reducing industrious, sober men to thievery

1

and black-market speculation and decent housewives and tender young girls to prostitution. It corrupts all political, social, and moral standards.

But we never have had galloping inflation in the United States. We have had a number of boom-and-bust cycles and many financial panics—plus one great humiliating depression that began on an October day in 1929 and lasted ten years, right into World War II.

We have seen greenbacks, fiat money issued by banks without government backing, become virtually worthless and, of course, the Confederacy issued a lot of money that lost value rapidly as the South's military fortunes waned in the Civil War.

But the real United States dollar, the one backed by gold and silver, by the financial sinews of the Federal Reserve banks, never has known a day of genuine weakness in terms of the currencies of other nations. We devalued its gold content in 1933 from $16.75 to the ounce to $35 an ounce—but that did not result in a weak dollar or in any price inflation to speak of. In fact, neither prices nor wages went up nearly as fast following the 1933 devaluation as President Franklin Delano Roosevelt probably hoped they would.

Consequently, unlike those who have lived through uncontrolled inflation in other countries, the great mass of Americans have very little accurate knowledge about inflation of any kind, galloping, uncontrolled, insidious, creeping—whatever adjective you want to apply to the phenomenon. But most of us shudder when we hear the word *inflation*. We think of it about as we think of Asiatic cholera or bubonic plague, those terrible diseases that kill so dramatically and so horribly and are no respecters of persons, races, colors, creeds or social classes.

We all have read about inflation in our school text-books. We see the word every day in the newspapers and hear it constantly on television and on the radio. We hear hundreds of alarums about it, hundreds of supposedly learned opinions about what causes inflation and how to avoid it or control it, from politicians, bankers, economists, teachers, industrialists and editors, and from a vast horde of crackpots.

Unfortunately, most of what we read or hear about inflation is highly charged with emotion. Even supposedly objective and scholarly academic economists can become very emotional and adopt a highly argumentative style when they talk about inflation. Perhaps this book also will sound polemical to many readers. I do have a point of view about inflation and I intend to expound it and defend it vigorously.

I am not an economist. However, I was born the year woman suffrage became a part of American life, and I grew up in the roaring twenties and the terrible years of the Great Depression. And having spent almost a quarter of a century in the insurance brokerage and securities brokerage business, I have had an unusually ample opportunity to see how creeping inflation and price cycles affect the lives of families and individuals and to observe how little most people comprehend the forces that affect prices and their paychecks.

My work has made it necessary to look into the lives of

thousands of families in our country and many other countries and to work with organizations interested in family welfare problems and the problem of developing an estate. I also have been called on to serve as financial adviser on insurance and other matters to many corporations and other financial institutions.

My purpose is to acquaint ordinary folk with what is known and believed to be true about inflation, in terms that will interest any ordinary man, housewife, or teenager.

If I have an ax to grind, it is simply to dispel fears about the specter of inflation. One of our greatest Presidents—it was the same one who found it necessary to halve the gold content of the dollar—once told us that Americans had and never would have anything to fear but fear itself. That is the attitude I believe we should take about the present inflationary problem—I hesitate to call it a peril, as so many people who should know better have done.

In the final chapter of a previous book,* written before the current inflation stirred public interest widely, I pointed out that creeping inflation of money and prices is inevitable and has been going on for centuries. This is the case because the material conditions of life improve steadily over the centuries, and this improvement has to be paid for. Inflation of money is, in the long run, the only way we have of paying for progress.

---

* *How to Get a Dollar's Value for a Dollar Spent* (New York, Citadel Press, 1964).

Our planet does not contain anything on which we can put a constant value forever. Gold is the nearest thing we have but there never was enough gold to go around. So the supposedly constant value of gold has had to be changed many times and has been maintained for comparatively short periods only with great difficulty.

The consequences of galloping inflation are dire indeed, and even creeping inflation, when it becomes sufficient in degree to be quite noticeable, hits some people very hard. Pensioners, people who live on Social Security payments, unemployables who are on relief, persons who live on annuities, and those workers whose skills are slight and whose bargaining power, individual or collective, consequently is weak are badly squeezed.

Nevertheless, history shows that society in general has prospered in periods of rising prices even though the rise was due to inflation as much as to upgrading of the quality of products by technological advance. Society even seems nearly always to have been able to make great economic, scientific and social strides right in the midst of severe inflationary conditions.

On the other hand, a study of most, but not all, of the periods when money and prices remained comparatively stable shows that scientific, economic and social progress usually slowed down. There was much economic and social progress in the stable-money eras of the nineteenth century. But even in that busy century, more progress occurred in the decades when prices and wages were rising. In the previous centuries, when prices and wages were firmly fixed by royal decree, man made very slow progress in any field—economic, scientific, social or political.

Many historians have wondered how the princes and archbishops of medieval Europe managed to finance the construction of their vast palaces and the great cathedrals out of an economy that was admittedly primitive and a social organization that had very little financial skill. Competent scholars recently have come up with a theory based on historical fact that they believe answers this question.

In the twelfth and thirteenth centuries, they have discovered, Europe was remarkably prosperous. Apparently the prosperity was brought about to a considerable degree by a practice called seigniorage;† a system of reissuing gold and silver coin periodically with a heavy tax, 10 percent or more, levied for reminting. The effect of the seigniorage tax was to make hoarding money impractical and to force all the coinage into circulation. Hoarded coins would lose value just as hoarded paper money will lose value today. Seigniorage was, in effect, a system of controlled inflation, and apparently it worked extremely well.

Why was seigniorage abandoned? I quote from my earlier book:

> According to the historians, the process was totally misunderstood by the people and there was constant clamor for its abolition and the introduction of permanent money. The barons and very rich feared that the

---

† *Seigniorage:* Any right or privilege or taxing power enjoyed by a feudal lord.

masses were becoming too prosperous and that what they regarded as the natural order of society would be subverted.

So the barons and the rich had their way. Seigniorage was abolished, the values of money and the prices of goods were generally frozen, trade languished and monopolies flourished, and Europe began a period of centuries of relative poverty while rulers and bankers sat on the lid trying to prevent the natural slow inflationary trend of history.

That medieval men misunderstood the workings of seigniorage should not astonish us. It must have seemed to them to be just another example of the debasing of the coinage resorted to so often in both the medieval and ancient worlds by extravagant tyrants to pay for their wasteful spending and their wasteful wars, and to consolidate their power. But there was a difference. The rulers who simply debased the coinage for their own ends either hoarded the gold they clipped or melted the coins and stole the profit or spent it on wasteful wars. On the other hand, the seigniorage tax was fed into the economy for useful purposes and served to prime the pumps or provide new mercantile and manufacturing capital, to create jobs and raise the standard of living.

Galloping inflation usually has been a reflex of war, but not always. Financial panics, accompanied by inflation, also have resulted from natural disasters such as floods, protracted drought and epidemics of cholera, and from irrational speculative fever—such as the South Seas Bubble, John Law's Mississippi Bubble and Holland's Tulip Bubble. The vast amounts of gold and silver plundered from the Indians in the Americas and brought to Europe in the sixteenth century caused much inflation.

In sketching briefly the modern story of inflation, probably a good place to start is the end of the Napoleonic wars in 1815. The destruction created in these conflicts naturally resulted in a lot of sporadic inflation, but in the fifteen years after Waterloo prices generally fell in western Europe and in the infant countries of the Americas. Then they moved slowly upward for forty years, accompanied by occasional money panics and brief interludes of severe deflation of prices.

After the defeat of France by Prussia in 1870, there was another brief series of panics, then prices remained relatively stable for another forty-five years until World War I. This period of stability saw much industrial and social progress, but nothing nearly so rapid as the progress in the later inflationary eras.

Some economists estimate that the net inflationary rise of prices from the final defeat of Napoleon to World War I was only 20 percent. They could be right, because the great Industrial Revolution enormously increased output in those years, and this huge increase in available goods was a counter-influence to normal inflation. Also, organized labor made very little advance in this period. Strikes occurred, but the strikers failed in their objectives more often than they won, so the workingman's productivity increased rapidly while his wages and standard of living went up very slowly.

The two world wars brought severe creeping inflation everywhere, and the aftermath of each war brought the most horrible kinds of uncontrolled inflation in many lands. We will discuss the nightmarish galloping inflation later.

We are inclined to talk about the Roaring Twenties as an era of great prosperity and extravagance, "the era of wonderful nonsense," but sober economic historians say the net economic trend of the decade of the 1920s was deflationary by a small margin. The 1930s, as even grade-school children know, brought the most severe deflation in all recorded history. Prices fell to rock bottom, businesses were bowled over like tenpins. Unemployment in the United States reached a nightmarish 30 percent or more of the working force. Hunger and frustration were rampant everywhere during the first four years of the 1930s, and the New Deal policies of President Roosevelt made what then seemed like snail's pace progress in restoring a semblance of prosperity. The rest of the world suffered even worse deflation and stagnation than Americans.

The severe dislocations and inflation of World War II were followed by widespread currency devaluations in 1949 except in North America, but contrary to the experience of the 1920s, these devaluations were not followed by either slow deflation or relative price and monetary stability. On the contrary, it was noticeable to observant economists that the historic long-term upward trend of prices had accelerated. Long-term inflation now walked instead of creeping.

New kinds of inflation were occurring. There was great argument about this then, and there has been ever since.

How much of this acceleration of prices was due to upgrading of true values in the economy—better products and services? How much was due to the newly imposed obligation of governments to provide full employment at all times? And how much was caused by timidity and irresponsibility of governments, of money managers, labor leaders and the public? But a most important question seldom was asked.

As early as the late 1890s, some more advanced economists had noted the inflationary impact of the new financial phenomenon of capitalizing assets, including all debts, on their earning power only. But few people understood this, so rarely was the question asked, How much had this new concept of capital accelerated the natural inflationary sources of society?

I'll take a good look at this phenomenon in later chapters.

2.

TOO MANY DOLLARS ABROAD

Although prices began rising before the escalation of the war in Vietnam, it was a succession of large deficits in our international balance of payments that really made Americans worry about the dollar.

The deficits started before our burden became so heavy in Southeast Asia. They resulted from the cost of our globe-girdling military commitments and the continuance of the foreign aid program. But foreign aid is regarded by most Americans as a moral obligation to peoples less fortunate than ourselves, as well as the most effective means of containing the expansion of Communist tyranny. The race with the Russians to explore outer space added strain to the national economy, but not to our international financial relations. During all the years that balance of payments deficits have plagued us, the United States has continued to enjoy a substantial balance of commerical exports over imports. But that favorable balance has been diminishing.

Of course, during these years we have had price-wage spirals at home that have been denounced in many quarters as being inflationary. Somehow, though, the mounting wages and other costs managed to be offset by the increasing productivity of the American worker and by the marvelous scientific, industrial and marketing technology of the nation. Of course, not everyone was convinced that price–wage inflation was being successfully counteracted. A little later we will talk about that and about cost–push or full-employment inflation.

A minor but annoying cause of pressure on the dollar abroad is counterfeiting. Many millions of bogus dollars are floating around Europe and Asia and, so long as they go undetected, they are claims against the United States' monetary gold stock and add to the balance of payments problem.

The German and Japanese governments counterfeited dollars during World War II. After the war, some of our so-called allied Communist governments also had the gall to print counterfeit dollars and use them to buy American goods.

Most of these early counterfeits have been detected and have disappeared, but new issues keep cropping up in substantial amounts. Some still are believed to be printed and floated by the intelligence agencies of Communist governments, particularly of Red China. Most, though, are the work of ordinary criminal counterfeiters. Some of these rings produce the bogus money in the United States and smuggle it to Europe and Asia, where it is put in circulation and used to buy up large quantities of better-grade foreign currencies, securities and easily negotiable merchandise. For example, Treasury agents caught a courier preparing to take off for India with two million counterfeit dollars printed in the United States.

Military scrip is used instead of dollars by our armed forces in combat zones in order to keep from increasing the number of dollars abroad, and while this scrip is a legal obligation of the United States, it cannot be redeemed in gold so cannot exercise a directly adverse effect on the balance of payments.

What turned out to be a more important cause of continuing balance of payments deficits was the enormous expansion of American business abroad, necessitating direct and indirect dollar investments in many countries on a vast scale. The nature of many of the most important industries that serve mankind is such that, in modern times, it takes large international corporations to produce and distribute goods with maximum efficiency. As the Western world's largest reservoir of capital and know-how, the United States had to play a leading role in this internationalization of business.

But the investments this required forced us to send abroad so many dollars that would not be coming home soon that our balance of payments was severely strained. Even if, as usually is the case, the foreign investment results in a substantial profit, neither the profits nor the exported capital can be repatriated to the United States soon. They are needed in the host countries to help bolster their economies. Nor do the American private investors have any overwhelming incentive to repatriate the dollars and other currencies they hold abroad and pay United States income or capital-gain taxes on them.

Obviously, much more is involved in the continuing balance of payments deficits than creeping inflation at home. It is not even certain that the balance of payments deficits contribute substantially to inflation at home. Rather, worry about the stability of the dollar in international transactions is a sign of our concern that we are dangerously overextended in our military, political and economic commitments abroad.

There are just too many United States dollars in circulation abroad—all of them claims against what is left of our Fort Knox gold hoard.

Sober-minded Americans are compelled to concede that no early ending of these commitments is in sight. Our burden in Europe has been reduced a little; if we could achieve peace in Vietnam, we would further reduce our commitments somewhat, but we still would be quite extended and new demands would be made upon us constantly for help for which American taxpayers would have to pay. The Communists are not going to let us off the hook—they are going to step up the rivalry whenever they can.

I do not pretend to be expert on the balance of payments. I will present only the salient facts. Anyone wanting a detailed discussion of the matter would do well to read *The Dollar and World Liquidity** by Robert V.

---

* *The Dollar and World Liquidity* (New York, Random House, 1967).

Roosa, our former Under Secretary of the Treasury, who has played an important official role in the efforts to keep the deficits down. Roosa's book has an appendix including digests of many of the relevant documents on the subject.

Roosa also expounds a point of view about the deficits. He says they are very dangerous to our national welfare, and we are not doing enough about the menace. He says we should be expanding our economy and restructuring our political and socio-economic system to make it more efficient so we can compete more effectively with the Communist world. In other words, we must beat the Communists at their own game. This implies acceptance of a degree of government planning that is unpalatable to Americans. But wars and deficits also are unpalatable.

The large American investments in the economies of other advanced nations have been greeted with very mixed feelings around the world. The people of the underdeveloped countries, who need American capital in ever larger amounts, are chagrined that American business preferred to invest in Europe rather than in their lands.

For the most part, European businessmen were eager enough to sell substantial interests in their companies to American firms who had the capital and know-how to make them grow more rapidly and produce more, creating more jobs and earning more profits.

But not all Europeans were happy about it. Some were very unhappy about the mushrooming growth of American investment in Europe and the accompanying spread of American cultural influence in their countries.

In particular, French President Charles de Gaulle did not like it. De Gaulle not only disliked the growing American stake in French industry and commerce but, as a traditionalist, he also disliked the whole trend of United States fiscal policy and the international monetary policy the Western world has followed since World War II under American leadership. The obstinate and somewhat mystical French leader appeared quite sincerely convinced that we Americans were leading the entire Western world down the path to financial and political ruin because of what he considered to be our irrational fear of Communist expansionism. He seemed to think we should have confidence in American ability, as he has in French ability, to coexist with the Communists without military confrontations and without resorting to new-fangled international financial arrangements that de Gaulle believed could only lead to disaster.

That is one view of *le roi* Charles. But not all Americans accepted this picture of de Gaulle. Those who did not accept it considered the French president a base ingrate, an arrogant hypocrite and either a dupe of the Communists, a man warped by corrosive hatred of the English-speaking world, or a cynical megalomaniac.

Both those Americans who accepted the first and kinder view of de Gaulle and those who had no patience with him were very annoyed with him. Both groups found his harsh, unsympathetic attitude on Vietnam particularly difficult to take, considering that we inherited the whole horrendous Vietnamese nightmare from the French, who misruled the country outrageously for generations and finally got thrown out by Ho Chi Minh.

De Gaulle's attacks on American economic policy and the suspicion that his government had engaged in deliberate clandestine machinations designed to aggravate our balance of payments deficit problems are equally distasteful to many Americans who remember that France still owes us approximately $6.7 billion she borrowed during World War I and later defaulted on.

De Gaulle's ambivalent attitude toward the United States and Britain—I find it difficult to believe he really hates us—goes back to World War II. In those days, he was just a scholarly, idealistic and somewhat romantic soldier. He had acquired none of the political finesse that he has displayed so brilliantly in recent years. He found it impossible to get along with such worldly realists as Franklin Roosevelt and Winston Churchill, and they found him extremely stiff-necked and imbued with a troublesome mystique. In consequence, de Gaulle was humiliated by the English-speaking leaders in those days to a degree that he cannot forget or forgive. In particular, he was humiliated when Roosevelt and Churchill chose first Admiral Darlan and then General Giraud, both of whom had collaborated with Marshal Petain's Vichy regime, over him as the French leader in liberated Algeria.

Nevertheless, there are qualities in de Gaulle that Americans must admire. He has done more for France than any French statesman in a century, and he is determined to restore France to the first rank among nations. Also, he stands firmly for peace in the world and he liquidated France's unprofitable and unjustly oppressive colonial empire in the face of bitter opposition from the feudal *colons* and the reactionaries at home—something no other French politician had the courage or ability to do.

At any rate, it was Charles de Gaulle who made Americans begin to worry about the stability of the dollar and to start asking if creeping inflation really was perilous.

De Gaulle thus forced us to think seriously for the first time since 1933 about whether the price of gold again should be raised and about whether we should take the lead in persuading the free world to abandon gold entirely as a monetary base.

France and the other nations that had accumulated huge quantities of dollars found it increasingly difficult to make use of the surplus dollars. They began to feel, with considerable justification in the eyes even of some Americans, that the $35 an ounce price for gold is grossly inadequate today.

Perhaps they would not have felt this way if they could have continued indefinitely to buy gold from our Fort Knox hoard at $35. Why should they want to pay us more for the gold than the price at which we are officially committed to sell to all customers? But the coin had a reverse side. These nations also held gold of their own and they came to believe that an ounce of their gold was worth a lot more than thirty-five United States paper dollars.

What really upset them, though, was the gradual development and substitution of what came to be known as the international gold exchange standard for the old-fashioned automatic gold standard. This is a system initiated by the United States in recent years to protect the stability of currencies in the face of the pressures of the cold war. There is no need to describe all its workings here in detail; it involves the international gold pool of six nations—France was a seventh partner until she withdrew—and a larger group of nations, including the six, who exchange large sums of their currencies among each other to create stabilization funds. It also involves voluntary or tacit agreements by the central banks of all these countries to refrain from drawing on each other's gold reserves heavily enough to force currency devaluation or to threaten the $35 an ounce gold price.

De Gaulle did not like these arrangements. He and his finance minister charged that they were simply a scheme to enable the United States to engage in reckless fiscal and financial irresponsibility in order to finance the war in Vietnam, and to "export inflation" to Europe by enabling American companies to buy up European businesses, particularly French companies, at bargain prices in inflated dollars. There is some merit to de Gaulle's accusations about the financial activities of American business in France, but the weight of sober opinion is that he has exaggerated the impact of American investment in France in order to make political capital.

An essential original feature of the gold exchange standard system was that it gave the dollar and the

British pound the status of reserve currencies in international transactions. International balances could be settled in dollars or pounds as well as in gold. De Gaulle set out to force the free world to abandon the use of the dollar and the pound as reserve currencies and to return to the old automatic gold standard under which all international balances were settled in gold coin or bullion.

De Gaulle's aim in this was by no means solely economic. His most important aim was political—even romantic. He wanted to whittle down the dollar and the pound so that the prestige of the United States and Britain would diminish in the world and the United States would have to cut back sharply its military role and its global economic activity. He believed this automatically would restore to France most of the eminence and glory she enjoyed before her defeat by Prussia in 1870.

Undoubtedly, de Gaulle remembered with humiliation that the French franc tumbled in the early 1920s from five to the dollar to twenty-five to the dollar, and to several hundred to the dollar at the end of World War II. It was not until the French nation turned to de Gaulle for leadership in the late 1950s that the franc was returned to its par value of five to the dollar.

This was a monumental achievement by the austere and romantic soldier who has been accused of considering himself a reincarnation of Joan of Arc.

De Gaulle set out first to wreck the British pound as a reserve currency and succeeded. On November 18, 1967, Britain's Labor Party government finally had to devalue the pound from $2.80 to $2.40. De Gaulle did not have to take overt measures to wreck the pound. He simply blocked admission of Britain to the prosperous European Common Market and dragged his feet when Prime Minister Harold Wilson appealed for help to save the pound. But suspicion persisted that the French financiers, with de Gaulle's tacit approval, had engaged in clandestine financial warfare against the pound.

Devaluation of the pound touched off a tremendous wave of speculation in gold bullion in Paris, Zurich and London. The French were accused of being the chief speculators, but later evidence indicated the principal speculators were Arabs and Asians—in fact, the gold buyers were scattered all around the globe. But the aim of the speculators was clear enough. They hoped to drain enough gold out of Uncle Sam's hoard at Fort Knox to compel the United States to raise the official gold price to $70 or even $105 an ounce.

The French government did not hesitate to express its sympathy with the gold speculators openly. At the very height of the crisis, de Gaulle held a news conference, savagely accused the United States of irresponsible financial aggression, and demanded a return to the old automatic international gold standard. Other French officials talked eagerly of an early lifting of the gold price to at least $70.

3.

THE CROSS OF
GOLD AGAIN

If the French were the only important critics of our gold policy, Americans would have been able to dismiss the matter by considering that our monetary problems would solve themselves when we succeeded in ending the war in Vietnam.

But long before the escalation of the Asian bonfire, the Canadians, the South Africans and the other gold-producing nations were saying that the $35 price no longer made sense. Some American gold mining companies simply said they no longer could mine gold at $35 an ounce and quit. The Canadians were urging a price of $55 in the middle 1950s.

Indeed, there was a substantial minority in the United States who wanted to return to the automatic gold standard and end the restrictions on the private ownership of gold enacted in 1933.

There is another and probably growing American minority who wants to abandon gold as a base for money altogether. A few days after Britain devalued the pound, a group of university economists wrote a letter to *The New York Times* urging that the United States stop buying gold at $35 an ounce, and end all sales of gold from the Treasury's monetary stock. The group claimed the majority of academic economists agreed with them, but other university economists promptly answered their letter, declaring that the United States, Britain and other Western nations had very recently given convincing examples of the kind of lack of financial and fiscal self-discipline that causes the public everywhere to have more faith in gold than in statesmen.

A few days later, at the annual Congress of American Industry sponsored by the National Association of Manufacturers, two prominent speakers, President George S. Moore of the First National City Bank of New York and Economist George Kline Smith said flatly that the $35 an ounce gold price had become totally unrealistic. Moore pointed out that when the gold price was set in 1933, the standard industrial wage in the United States was about one dollar an hour. Today industrial wages are two and a half to five times that. Smith found it almost intolerable that man still cannot manage financial and economic affairs without resorting to gold as a measuring rod. Moore said an eventual large increase in the international price of gold could not be ruled out.

But having walked boldly thus far out on the limb, both speakers protected their rear and flank positions, and coppered all bets. They said that, for right now, they preferred to depend on fiscal and monetary self-discipline to curb inflation and solve the balance of payments deficit rather than raise the gold price.

Now, of course, even though raising the gold price could get the United States off the hook insofar as our immediate gold drain is concerned, that would only be treating the symptoms of the disease, and not getting at the cause. But if, as probably a majority of Americans believed at the time, the war in Vietnam were the root cause of our financial malaise, an absolute cure obviously would depend as much on the Communists as on ourselves. Nevertheless, Moore and Smith were quite correct in saying there was much that could be done to help the situation simply by means of self-discipline.

And even if the $35 gold price is highly unrealistic today, there seemed little reason to believe the United States could be harmed in the near future by defending it. The international gold speculators and President de Gaulle clearly were underestimating the strength of the American economy.

The matter was put in a nutshell by the Wall Street investment banking firm of Salomon Brothers & Hutzler, a house noted for the competence and thoroughness of its economic research department. The firm explained matters this way: "The status of the dollar in international finance is inadequately judged by reference only to our one quickest asset, monetary reserves." The banking house then suggested that American private claims on foreigners, long-term and short-term, totaled a gigantic $101 billion.

"Furthermore," the report said, "during the last three years, in spite of the deficits in our balance of payments, our assets of all sorts have been rising faster than our liabilities. Even our total short-term claims on foreigners of $29 billion are almost as large as our short-term external obligations."

Then suddenly something occurred to lend real drama to the whole question of inflation and gold. William Mc-Chesney Martin, Jr., the chairman of the Federal Reserve Board, who had been an open critic of the Johnson Administration's easy-money policies on several occasions, made a speech in Washington that was supposed to be off the record, but was not. A reporter from *The New York Times* declared he had been invited under false pretense and refused to accept the admonition that Martin was not to be quoted, and the *Times* printed Martin's remarks on the front page.

The remarks were worth it. The august and austere Chairman of the Federal Reserve Board of Governors called gold a "barbarous metal," which, in the eyes of traditionalists, was almost as heretical as saying God is a barbarian. Martin agreed wholeheartedly with George Kline Smith and the minority of university economists who had been preaching that it was monstrous that men still had to depend on gold as a money base. Specifically, Martin said he found it monstrous that the peoples of the free world still do not have enough faith in their governments' ability to manage monetary affairs safely without the archaic dependence on gold. Martin was throwing down the gauntlet to de Gaulle with a vengeance.

However, Martin's speech was not widely reported. Most of the news media decided to honor his request that it be off the record. Also, Americans today are rather shockproof. They are not likely to be electrified by what one man says, as they were back in 1896.

That was the year when the most dramatic, and possibly still the most important, speech in history on the subject of gold and inflation was made. I am not the only modern American, interested in the money question, to turn back the pages of history to see what was in that famous speech. The speech tells us a lot. Reading it reminds us that, although we never had serious inflation in the United States on a national scale in the past, only local greenback inflation, still the gold standard has been under intermittent attack throughout our national history, and the question of the gold standard involves wider and deeper moral and social issues than the momentary stability of the dollar.

The 1896 speech was made by William Jennings Bryan, a comparatively young congressman from Nebraska, at the Democratic National Convention. It won him the Presidential nomination. Bryan was espousing easy money based on bimetallism, the free coinage of silver with silver to be priced officially at one-sixteenth the price of gold. Bryan was defeated for the Presidency by William McKinley, a quiet, ruthless imperialist from Ohio, who was the darling of Wall Street. McKinley's administration crushed the agrarian and working class population by means of a mountainous tariff wall that gave every manufacturer, railroad operator and banker in the country a license to commit wholesale plunder. McKinley also turned our war against Spain from an idealistic struggle to liberate the oppressed Cubans into a colonial territorial grab that played a big part in involving us in war with Japan forty years later. So, indirectly we can trace our troubles in Vietnam back to McKinley, too. If he had not involved us in a prolonged stay in the Philippines, we might never have become deeply enough involved anywhere in Asia to get into conflicts in Korea and Vietnam. However, McKinley's immediate successor, Theodore Roosevelt, and Roosevelt's cronies, John Hay, the elder Henry Cabot Lodge and Senator Albert Beveridge of Indiana, the apostle of "manifest destiny," were far more to blame than McKinley for our Asian involvement.

But historians revealed McKinley long ago. We are more interested in remembering what his opponent said about what later became the main issue of the 1896 campaign, the gold standard. Bryan was addressing the Democrats, but he was hurling defiance at Wall Street and at the business oligarchies of Boston, Philadelphia, Pittsburgh and Chicago. Here is the pertinent and most famous passage in that 1896 speech:

> We say to you that you have made the definition of a businessman too limited in its application. The man who is employed for wages is as much a businessman as his employer . . . the miners who go down a thousand feet into the earth . . . and bring forth from their hiding

places the precious metals to be poured into the channels of trade are as much businessmen as the few financial magnates who, in a back room, corner the money of the world. We come to speak of this broader class of businessmen. . . . You shall not press down upon the brow of labor this crown of thorns. You shall not crucify mankind upon a cross of gold.

Bryan never made it into the White House, although the Democrats nominated him three times, but his ideas triumphed. He did not win free coinage of silver at sixteen to one. The vested money powers of the nation considered that our western states could produce too much newly mined silver to make that bearable. But the United States Treasury did mint millions of silver dollars and issued many paper silver certificates against stored silver bars. Bryan and his followers believed so strongly in silver money because China and other Asian nations had used silver as their main monetary base for centuries with great success.

But Bryan's ringing eloquence stung the consciences of the English-speaking world. Gradually, during the next forty years, academic economists, historians, statesmen and even bankers began to realize that, in fact, monarchs, aristocrats and plutocrats had crucified the commonalty of mankind on a cross of gold for centuries.

What would happen if the United States suddenly decided not only to "suspend specie payments," but to cut all ties between the dollar and gold?

In his speech to the NAM Business Congress, President George Moore of First National City Bank admitted he did not know what would happen in that event, but that he suspected whatever did happen would be bad. And we have seen that the academic economists are very divided in their views of what would happen. Of one thing we can be sure: The outcome would depend not on any supposedly natural law of economics, but solely on human opinion.

Almost two thousand years ago, the philosopher emperor of Rome, Marcus Aurelius, who still is regarded as one of the better thinkers of all time, said the most important thing he had learned in his life was that "there is no reality in the universe except opinion." Marcus Aurelius could afford to make this observation, implying as it did that even the gods owed their importance entirely to human opinion; as Caesar, he also was ex officio Pontifex Maximus with the power to alter religious dogma, and even to proclaim himself a god if he wished. A whole succession of lesser caesars had done just that.

Thus, the future of the dollar if it were cut completely loose from gold would depend on what people, Americans and foreigners, thought about it. If people continued to think the dollar strong, it would remain strong, and gold, after first going up in price, might later drop in value very sharply. Someone has figured out that if gold no longer were used as a monetary base by the major nations, its value for industrial, scientific and dental use, and even for jewelry, would be less than $10 an ounce. That is much less than the cost of mining new gold today, so all the gold-mining companies in the world would automatically be out of business. It is doubtful, though, that the gold-mining companies would go broke. They are highly solvent and are run by able men. They would find new businesses to enter just as the Suez Canal Company easily converted itself into a diversified industrial and financial enterprise after President Nasser of Egypt took over the Canal.

As for metallic gold, it is an almost indestructible metal and a great deal of it has been accumulated around the world. It might be some time before industry and science began to feel a gold shortage, for gold is not as valuable as a utilitarian metal as silver. One reason the United States finally stopped issuing silver dollars and silver certificates is that silver eventually became worth more to the metallurgical and chemical industries than its official monetary value. Speculators were melting down silver dollars and cashing in silver certificates to get silver to sell to industry.

One nation whose opinion on the gold question is quite important is the Soviet Union. The Soviet Government very recently showed how it is thinking. The Kremlin announced in mid-December, 1967, that Russia, already one of the world's big producers of newly mined gold, would step up gold exploration and mining. The Kremlin evidently did not believe the United States would demonetize gold, but probably hoped, along with the French, the Canadians, the South Africans and some other governments, that Washington eventually would be compelled by the logic of events to accept a big increase in the gold price.

And how would that affect us? It would be a blow to our pride and prestige, and it could come at a particularly inconvenient time—when we are politically and diplomatically, if not militarily, overextended in the world. Unless all the countries in the world immediately followed us in raising the gold price, we should have to pay more dollars for what we imported and we would get considerably fewer dollars for everything we exported.

However, the interests of most nations in the world undoubtedly would be best served by following our example and devaluing their currencies in terms of gold, so things might stay very much as they are. There might be no acceleration whatsoever of the creeping inflation here at home.

The Soviet Union and the other Communist countries might have considerable incentive not to follow our lead, and not to devalue their currencies. If they did not, the Russian ruble would become worth considerably more in relation to the dollar than it is now. The Russians might be able to make considerable diplomatic and propaganda capital out of that, and the higher value of the ruble might enable the Soviet bloc to strengthen its relative economic weight in the world even faster than it has in the past decade. The ruble is nominally worth about the same as the dollar, but the Soviet Government, with a completely managed economy and no speculative free enterprise allowed within its sphere, maintains several different official prices for the ruble for domestic trade, tourist trade, ordinary commercial foreign trade and special bilateral trade arrangements. Also, the Russians subordinate trade and finance so utterly to political and diplomatic considerations that it is difficult for an ordinary American businessman to hazard a guess as to what they really would do.

The only thing we know for sure about this question is that, ever since Josef Stalin's death, the Soviet state and Soviet banking and industrial enterprises have become much more sophisticated in economics. This, coupled with the fact that they have demonstrated by their successes in the space race that they are capable of harnessing their energies and scientific skills on a vast scale very rapidly and successfully, should lead us to believe that whatever they would do about a world-wide monetary change or revolution would be done wisely and efficiently and would serve Russia's interest and the Communist cause well.

4.

GALLOPING
INFLATION

Properly speaking, there could be little
money inflation in the ancient world because there was
no currency to inflate.

The crudely minted gold, silver and copper coins were
accepted on their intrinsic metallic value. Of course,
prices could and did rise fantastically in the wake of war,
famine, pestilence or other disaster. But the amount of
money in circulation rarely could be expanded rapidly
in the way that the amount of gold coin in circulation in
Europe was expanded to inflationary levels in the sixteenth century when the Spaniards brought so much gold
from the Americas—a large proportion of which was cap-
tured on the high seas by Drake, Raleigh and other English pirates commissioned by Elizabeth I.

But when prices rose rapidly in the ancient world,
the resulting hardship was far worse than anything we
could imagine today. The poor starved to death by the

thousands. Those who did not die were sold into slavery to pay off paltry debts. Men sold first their daughters and sisters, then their sons and wives, and finally themselves as slaves in order to eat.

We have already seen how princes periodically debased the coinage in order to steal from their subjects and how this finally developed into the practical system of financing social progress known as seigniorage in the Middle Ages.

Meanwhile, the Chinese had invented currency, paper notes and small copper coins backed by silver bars stored in vaults. Marco Polo, the thirteenth-century Venetian who was the first European to travel in China and write about the country, was astonished to find the Chinese using pieces of vermilion paper inscribed with characters for money in place of gold and silver. The Chinese assured him that the paper money was readily acceptable and kept its value, but Marco Polo had a healthy skepticism of mind. He kept asking questions and learned that the paper money sometimes was repudiated or lost nearly all its value through inflation in time of war or famine or simply because of the skulduggery or incompetence of the emperor's officials.

Apparently, periodic inflation in medieval China could be either mild or drastic. But since Chinese civilization was entirely feudal and the economy based on self-sustaining family and village units, the paper currency was regarded more as a convenient substitute for barter than as real wealth; when paper money lost its value, it was easy enough to slip back into a barter economy until conditions improved. Thus, the money inflation scarcely could have any serious consequences even if it were of the galloping variety. The scarcity of food and other goods that caused the inflation could cause hardship, but not the inflation itself.

But this is far from being true of galloping inflation as it has been known in the West. In Western countries, galloping inflation has been a reflex of extreme scarcity, all right, but usually there have been complications of a political or psychological nature so severe that they probably can be considered more important than actual scarcity of commodities.

Take the comparatively recent galloping inflationary experiences in Argentina, Brazil and Uruguay. Argentina's economy was wrecked by a fascist dictator who was greedy, unbelievably inept, absurdly impatient and ridden by an insensate hatred of the agricultural–financial oligarchy that owned and operated the country's only important industry—cattle and meat. Juan Perón deliberately disrupted the Argentine meat industry in order to vent his hatred of the landed aristocracy. He was too impatient to fight it out slowly with the aristocrats, and preserve the country's economic life blood, so he inflated wages and the peso at a galloping rate in order to win labor as an ally against the oligarchy.

Inflation in Brazil also is associated with a fascist dictator, the late Getulio Vargas, and a succession of other demagogic political leaders. But the truth is that Brazil always has lived on the edge of inflationary disaster for an amazing variety of reasons. In spite of her great size and potential strength, Brazil is a nation singularly disadvantaged by nature and history. Few nations have had such formidable geographic, climatic, demographic and social obstacles to overcome. Large-scale illiteracy, miserable health standards and a well-nigh incredible greediness and callousness on the part of the propertied classes, are the main elements of the Brazilian picture.

The inflation in Uruguay is attributed to almost exactly opposite causes. One of the most progressive democracies in the world, Uruguay was extremely prosperous by Latin American standards until very recent years. There were virtually no illiteracy, no demagoguery, only remarkable stability and progress for almost a century. But like many other Latin American countries, Uruguay's economy depended on agricultural products, meat, leather and wool. For a generation now, producers of such basic commodities have found themselves at a great disadvantage in world markets in dealing with industrialized countries, particularly if they produce natural substances such as leather and wool that have been displaced increasingly by synthetics.

Yet inflation was not inflicted on Uruguay either by scarcity or by the ineptitude or the megalomania of a dictator. Rather, it resulted from creeping anarchy. A cradle-to-the-grave welfare state, the fact that almost one-third of the populace was on the government payroll, and the agitative activity of a small hard-core Communist party started the inflation by repeated waves of strikes that disastrously interfered with production in what is, after all, a marginal economy at best. A Swiss-style national council government with no executive branch vested with real power to rule or guide facilitated the drift toward chaos and economic anarchy. Floods, drought and a disastrous winter that ruined the vital fodder crop for the cattle industry provided the knockout blow.

Americans can draw lessons from Uruguay's galloping inflation. Even a model economy can blow up in inflation if everybody behaves irresponsibly and there is no one at the helm to swing the tiller in the right direction.

Whatever its causes, galloping inflation always results in terrible hardship and demoralization and, more often than not, it takes many years to restore an economy crippled by drastic inflation.

Galloping inflation need not be associated with real scarcity at all. South Vietnam experienced a most demoralizing galloping inflation due to the tidal wave of American dollars spent in the country to support the war effort. The amount of money in circulation in South Vietnam went up sevenfold in six years, and prices in Saigon and the other cities skyrocketed fantastically. Luxury apartment houses, hotels, fancy shops and restaurants, new factories and impressive public buildings were put up right in the midst of the war. Everybody speculated and everybody had money. There was a great deal more money than goods, but still goods were not really scarce. The streets were filled with new automobiles. One could buy anything in Saigon that could be bought anywhere in the world. The material standard of living in the capital was high even for the working class.

Yet, only a few miles away in the jungle villages, the peasants lived much as they always have by subsistence farming, also right in the midst of the war. This is one very important aspect of wartime inflationary prosperity in South Vietnam that should concern us—the peasant did not share in it. Partly because the Vietcong interdicted him from shipping his rice to the cities and partly because the South Vietnamese government would not pay the peasant a price for rice commensurate with the inflation going on in the country, the peasants grew only enough rice for their own use. In consequence, whereas for generations South Vietnam had been a net exporter of rice to the rest of Asia, she soon began to import almost one million tons a year! This sorry situation hardly was conducive to making the South Vietnamese peasantry more willing to fight for the Saigon government or for the Americans, who looked to him suspiciously like the French oppressors who ruled the country so long and so badly. The stench of social and political corruption in Saigon caused by the inflationary prosperity was all-pervading, according to Americans who have spent some time in the country. Apparently none of the Saigonese or the hundreds of thousands of other South Vietnamese who drifted into the capital could resist it. Everyone, from young children to wrinkled grandparents, was engaged in some kind of black-marketing, thievery or prostitution. But the Vietnamese did not delude themselves; they knew they were being corrupted by the inflation, and because they are essentially a proud people with a culture, a philosophy and moral unity going back at least

a thousand years, they felt guilty about allowing themselves to be corrupted by the flood of easy American
money. It made many of them loathe us in precisely the
same way that a high-priced harlot, who is innately a
sensitive person, loathes her patrons even as she strives
to please them. The inflation we imported into Vietnam,
instead of buying us friends, frequently bought us hatred
and new enemies.

On the other hand, the Vietcong managed to win the
respect and even the admiration of the peasants in spite
of their hideous cruelty because of their spartan frugality
and their puritanical fanaticism.

The two world wars in our century have brought
general waves of galloping inflation in Europe, and
World War II bowled over the currencies of much of
Asia as well. These inflationary experiences all resulted
from genuine scarcity of goods of all kinds, particularly
food. But in certain important respects, the uncontrolled
expansion of the currency differed from country to country. In Japan, for example, the downfall of the yen reflected thwarted ambition and collapsed hopes. On the
other hand, in France and Italy, the causes of the uncontrolled inflation, in addition to scarcity, were decades
of extremely backward, incompetent governments, underdeveloped industry, obsolete technology and propertied classes characterized mainly by ruthlessness, selfish-
ness and a firm conviction that, like the feudal aristocrats
of old, rich men should pay no taxes.

But the most spectacular inflation in Europe occurred
in Germany and Austria. Defeat, of course, was the pri-

mary cause, and the dismemberment of the Hapsburg empire left Austria resembling nothing so much as a pricked balloon. As .for Germany, the 1918 armistice plunged her overnight from being the second greatest power on earth to a third-rate republic, occupied by Allied armies, stripped of her navy and merchant marine and deprived by force of the export markets and sources of raw materials on which the empire had been built. But what crippled defeated Germany worst of all was the determination of the French to exact from her mountains of reparations in gold and goods for the damage France had sustained in the war, plus restitution and retribution for the harsh indemnity and partitioning Bismarck had imposed on France in 1870.

The United States and Britain sought to restrain the French to some extent, but with little success. The "Tiger," Georges Clemenceau, was premier of France; and Clemenceau was old enough to have personally experienced Prussian harshness in 1870. British losses in the war had been so heavy that Prime Minister David Lloyd George found it extremely difficult to get the average Englishman to listen to suggestions that it would be dangerous for the future of mankind to punish the Germans so severely as to drive the whole nation to despair. Indeed, the little Welshman found that sympathy for the Germans stuck in his own throat.

The Allies made it clear at once that Germany's reparations bill would be upwards of one hundred billion gold marks and that her access to choice foreign markets and sources of raw materials would remain severely limited for many years.

How then, asked the desperate statesmen of the infant German republic, would Germany ever earn the gold to pay the reparations bill? There was no answer that made sense. The stage thus was set for the great German drama of 1923.

5.

THE GERMAN DRAMA: AND JOHN LAW

The German imperial mark had a par or gold value of four to the dollar when gold was $16.75 an ounce. The mark retained its vigor throughout World War I, but deteriorated rapidly on the international market from the moment the armistice was signed, falling to 162 to the dollar.

It continued to slip steadily as jockeying for power by socialists, communists, extreme nationalists and various big business groups and veterans' organizations kept Germany on the verge of civil war. By 1922, it was down to 7,000 to the dollar, but this did not mean the mark's purchasing power at home had fallen anywhere near so low. Things were bad in Germany. Millions were jobless. People were not starving or freezing exactly, but they were very hungry all year and very cold each winter. Crime and corruption were rampant not only in the cities but throughout Germany. However, the Germans don't have to be encouraged to work; in fact, it is impossible to keep them from working if they can find anything at all to do, and they adore discipline. So the crippled home economy managed to struggle along and make a little progress, and the badly inflated mark still was a usable currency at home.

But there were many hundreds of millions of marks scattered around the world in bank vaults and in the hands of individuals that nobody could find any earthly use for because the Germans now had absolutely nothing to sell for marks.

In exchange for what they did have to sell—jewelry, art treasures, patents, technological and scientific skills and some important biologicals, pharmaceuticals and other chemicals—they had to demand payment in hard currencies, dollars, pounds, Swiss francs, Dutch guilders or Swedish crowns. That is why the imperial mark so quickly became practically worthless on the international market.

But the great inflation of 1923 that saw the mark drop to the astronomical figure of 4.2 trillion to the dollar (if you actually can visualize such a number) was triggered by the French. The Paris government became convinced, with some good reason, that the Germans were dragging their heels on production and deliveries of reparations in coal, steel and other important commodities. The French army of occupation was dramatically reinforced overnight and the rich Rhineland and Ruhr industrial areas were seized.

German Chancellor Wilhelm Cuno retaliated by ordering a total cessation of reparations. The French coun-
tered this move by cutting off the Rhineland and the
Ruhr completely from the rest of Germany, a move that
paralyzed virtually all German commerce and industry.
Prices rose so fast that the mark soon was as inflated at
home as it was abroad.

But the inflation did not stop there. With Teutonic
thoroughness and ruthlessness, the Germans proceeded
to wipe the financial slate clean no matter who got hurt.
The printing presses rumbled twenty-four hours a day
turning out notes in ever more fantastic denominations.
In no time, all the nongold domestic debt in Germany,
public and private, everything payable in paper marks,
was repudiated effectively by means of the astronomical
inflation. Mortgages, bonds, bank loans, contracts, accounts receivable, accounts payable, insurance policies,
not to mention all savings and bank deposits, annuities,
pensions—everything was wiped out! This was one galloping inflation in which not even the shrewdest and
boldest traders could make a profit out of the currency;
a profit of a billion marks made at ten in the morning
would be wiped out less than two hours later as the exchange ratio doubled again or even increased tenfold.
Of course, lots of speculators bought valuable properties
and goods for the worthless paper and kept them, but
those that resold at a profit in marks were instantly
ruined.

At the peak of the relentless output of the printing

presses, a German needed a wheelbarrow loaded with paper money to buy a loaf of bread!

Everything, of course, was totally out of kilter. Nobody any longer had the faintest idea what anything was worth or what the next hour would bring, much less the next day. Employers hadn't the faintest notion of how much wages to pay nor had workers any idea of how much they would need to survive through the next twenty-four hours.

Naturally, there were food riots everywhere and crime, already serious, multiplied tenfold.

In the middle of it all, a rather laconic news item reported that an ex-Wehrmacht corporal named Adolf Hitler and a handful of other rather seamy war veterans had staged a march from a beer hall in Munich in an attempt to seize control of the city government. The fantastic inflation brought the country closer to the brink of civil war, as Chancellor Cuno had foreseen. His government fell, but his amazing tactics forced Washington and London to put pressure on the French to show some common-sense restraint. Also, the Germans found two important new leaders, Dr. Gustav Stresemann, the scholarly diplomat, and Dr. Hjalmar Schacht, a financial wizard who became head of the Reichsbank and remained at the helm of German finances for twenty years, all through the Nazi era and World War II.

Banker Charles G. Dawes of Illinois, who later became Calvin Coolidge's Vice President, headed an international commission to work out a new German reparations plan, while Schacht created a new gold Reichsmark. It was exchanged for the old marks at a ratio of one to one trillion.

The creation of the new Reichsmark effectively "resurrected" much of the debts and assets wiped out in the runaway inflation—in the case, for example, of term obligations where the creditors had the legal right to refuse prepayment in the worthless inflated marks.

In her preoccupation with collecting reparations from the Germans, France neglected to put her own financial and economic house in order, and soon was ripe for runaway inflation also. Although the franc remained strong until the end of World War I, it lost half its value both on the domestic and international markets in 1918. Things got worse instead of better. By 1920 real wages in France were lower than in 1911 in spite of the fact that French industry and agriculture were running full blast; the French were having to recruit labor in Italy, Germany and Poland. French technology was backward, the bureaucracy inept and French business and government finances inefficient and hopelessly expensive. There was too much dependence on short-term loans and indirect taxation. The working classes and petite bourgeoisie paid almost all the taxes. Business, the professional classes and the wealthier landowners paid practically nothing. Gold hoarding, always a national vice in France, had accelerated. The government was engaged in the costly expansion of the colonial empire in North Africa, Indo-China (Vietnam, Cambodia and Laos), Syria and Madagascar, which earned enormous profits for a few

Frenchmen but was only a strategic and economic burden on the nation as a whole.

While the government could and did act swiftly and recklessly on external matters, it was almost impotent at home. The multiplicity of splinter parties, the selfish rigidity of the party cliques and the vast conglomeration of local special interests prevented any sensible reform. The inflation reached the runaway stage in 1925 when the franc dropped to almost fifty to the dollar, and at last many of the greediest and most predatory elements of the French populace and business world got their comeuppances. Parliament refused to give two successive premiers decree power to deal with the crisis, but finally, in 1926, gave in and permitted Raymond Poincare to stabilize the franc at twenty-five to the dollar.

There was a new wave of inflation in France in the 1930s and the franc had to be devalued again in 1937. The inflations between the two world wars scarred the soul of France deeply. It created bitter class hatreds because all Frenchmen know their country is naturally rich, and the only possible explanation historians can find for the humiliations and hardships they had to endure as a result of the inflation lies in human greed, cruelty and obstinacy.

The galloping inflation after World War II was more widespread and more directly based on scarcity of material goods. It was checked by the Marshall Plan help from the United States and by the rise of a number of rather capable governments in the countries involved.

From what we have observed, it is easy to see that

none of the conditions that cause galloping inflations exists in the United States today.

The most interesting runaway inflation in history is the "granddaddy" of them all—John Law's Mississippi Bubble, which bankrupted France in 1720 after having made multimillionaires of hundreds of speculators who were shrewd enough to convert their profits from trading in Mississippi shares into gold or land.

The Mississippi Bubble is important because it is the first case in European history of inflation of the currency itself; indeed, it marked the first time any European country had issued paper money to an important extent.

Even today, historians have difficulty deciding whether John Law was a swindler or simply a tragically mistaken genius. The greater weight of evidence tends to the second view. Certainly his contemporaries felt that way, because he never was prosecuted even though his operations ruined so many people. There can be no doubt that Law was a mathematical genius. He was a tall, handsome Scot from Edinburgh, romantic and dashing. By profession, he was a gambler. In the early eighteenth century a man who could make his living at cards and dice without resorting to cheating was held in the highest social esteem. Gambling was a respectable enough occupation for a nobleman or even a prince of the blood, while to be a tradesman or a lawyer or a physician was to be definitely ordinary.

John Law was possibly the most successful gambler who ever lived. He worked out for himself, a century ahead of any other mathematician, the numerical laws of probability and chance so accurately that he was simply unbeatable at the gaming tables. He made enormous sums gambling and thereby attracted the acquaintanceship of the most powerful noblemen in Europe. Even in his old age, when he was a broken man as a result of the collapse of the Mississippi Bubble, Law supported himself comfortably by gambling while living in retirement in Venice. In those last days, people were amazed to see him lay bets on the turn of the cards at odds as high as 20,000 to one—and win consistently. For he was the only man in Europe, the only man of his day, who really knew what the correct odds were. And he had a brain that calculated with something like the speed of a modern electronic computer.

When Law first became a social lion in Paris because of his dazzling skill at the gaming tables, France was facing utter financial ruin because of the wars and extravagances of the recently deceased King Louis XIV. Philippe d'Orleans, regent for the boy king Louis XV, sought Law's financial advice.

Law mulled the matter over and, in due time, came up with two schemes which eventually were merged into one after both had been put into effect. He would create a Bank of France to issue paper money redeemable in gold, but with very thin gold backing, and he would create a government-sponsored company with shares to be sold to the French public. In return for the exclusive right to exploit and develop the vast valley of the Mississippi River, which belonged to France all the way from Canada to the Gulf of Mexico, this company would take over the entire French national debt from the existing bondholders, paying them in stock, and would reduce the government's interest rate.

Philippe, and everybody else in France, fell for the plan, hook, line and sinker. Indeed, from such records as we have, it appears that the private bankers, princes and other moneyed men of Europe also thought the scheme was marvelous and were green with envy.

To us today, the whole plan seems incredibly naïve, but it was conceived and launched in a naïve era.

Philippe made Law comptroller of France and gave him virtually the powers of a prime minister in addition. Law launched both the bank and the company and soon had all France in a frenzy of speculation in shares of the Mississippi Company. The shares were originally issued at 500 livres and were swiftly pushed up to 28,000 livres! When the market started to collapse, Law suddenly demonetized gold and made it a crime to own gold in France.

Meanwhile, his Banque de France was printing fiat paper money at breakneck speed and pumping it into circulation to enable people to buy more stock in the Mississippi Company. The inflation was instantaneous; prices went up so fast that the cost of living rose sevenfold in Paris. But everybody was getting rich off the speculation, and everybody had to indulge in it. The only way for a Parisian to make enough money to keep up with rising prices was to speculate in Mississippi shares.

In degree, the Mississippi Bubble speculation makes anything we have ever seen in the United States seem pretty tame. At the height of the Bubble, it was not uncommon for scores of such ordinary people as valets and small shopkeepers to make profits to $100,000 (reckoned in today's money) in an afternoon! And many of the speculators salted away half or more of their winnings in gold, land or other valuable tangibles.

When the Bubble began to shrink, Law tried to convert the shares into fixed-priced securities at a liberal rate, in the hope that that would stop the public from selling them. It had the opposite effect. About the same time, Law tried to do something about the inflation by proposing to gradually revalue the livre. That did it. Instantly public opinion turned against him and then the panic was on. France was ruined financially, although many individuals had made huge fortunes.

Law was stunned by the turn of events. He could not understand how his system had failed. It is very easy for us to judge him harshly from the vantage point of two hundred and fifty years of accumulated professional knowledge of financial and economic management, but Law believed he was right.

Law discovered much more than the mathematical laws governing gambling. He proved the utility and superiority of paper money as an ordinary medium of exchange. He was the first financier in the world to discover the expansible nature of credit. Most of the Mississippi Company shares were sold on 10 percent margin.

Even his concept of a state-owned company to develop the Mississippi Valley was not without merit. The potential value of the vast region was enormous, but Law had no conception of what it would require in time, manpower and technology to develop the Louisiana territory, while Philippe the regent and the rest of the French were not interested; many actually were naïve and greedy enough to think Law had found a way to speculate forever without risk!

The French public had been induced to pour about $3 billion (in today's money) into a company to develop Louisiana. Yet a century later, when New Orleans had become a thriving city, Thomas Jefferson had no trouble talking Napoleon I into selling the whole Louisiana Territory to the infant American republic for $30 million in gold at today's prices.

There remains one footnote. When the Mississippi Bubble collapsed and Law was dismissed, Philippe the regent then committed one of the most astonishing acts of tyrannical double-crossing in history. Even though his government had sponsored the Mississippi Company and virtually forced people to speculate in the shares, Philippe issued a decree in July, 1721, ordering all commoners who had made profits from the speculations to yield them up to the state to the last penny as a fine for seeking to rise above their natural condition in life! The nobility was exempted.

This amazing decree was carried out to the letter. A small tradesman, who, perhaps, had prudently salvaged

10,000 livres from his speculative profits, was stripped to his undershirt, while the Duc de Bourbon, who had stashed away $50 million of such speculative gains, was allowed to keep it all. No one ever learned how much Philippe himself made out of the Bubble.

6.

INFLATION
AND JOBS

Business and academic economists call
typical modern creeping inflation "cost–push" inflation,
and say it has very little to do with monetary problems.

Rather, they say it arises from the political and social
obligation of governments to maintain full employment
of a working force that keeps expanding because the
life span keeps increasing and virtually all children grow
up to become workers.

As an experienced life insurance man, I am extremely
conscious of the impact of the population explosion, and
the fact that a childhood mortality that ran almost to 50
percent at the start of this century in the advanced countries has been nearly wiped out. But the effect of population explosion and a lengthened life span on the life
insurance business has been deflationary; it has caused
life insurance to become much less expensive.

Population explosion and the longer life span have

created bigger markets and greatly expanded production for all industries, but they have created unemployment problems such as the world never knew before; the efforts to solve these problems are certainly in part responsible for cost-push inflation.

The ancient world was not troubled too much by unemployment. We think of labor as being plentiful then because pay was low, but normally labor was scarce in the ancient world just as many other commodities were scarce. The rulers of the ancient world, in dealing with labor problems employed the most brutal of all means, and the most shortsighted means—slavery.

Slavery is shortsighted because it brutalizes the masters even more than the slaves and makes the whole population, both free and slave, apathetic and backward, incapable of giving birth to new ideas and improvements themselves and highly resistant to accepting new ideas or better methods from others. It also was highly wasteful in the ancient world. Slaves in those times rarely lived more than thirty-five years, so their productive life in proportion to their cost was pitifully short and uneconomic. But since the life span of free workers usually was equally short, the masters did not realize how wasteful slavery was.

Slavery did sometimes produce unemployment problems among free citizens. For many generations in the Roman Empire, the free working classes, tradesmen, peasants and such professional men as doctors and teachers, musicians, athletes and other performers could not compete with slave labor in their own fields. In consequence, the free common citizenry was reduced to living in stultifying idleness on caesar's dole, or to becoming soldiers or brigands.

Because they were treated so contemptuously and brutally that they died off like flies, there was rarely any surplus of slave labor, so no slave unemployment problem. When there was, the surplus slaves simply were butchered to get rid of them, and society continued to waste human resources deliberately.

Wars, pestilence, ordinary diseases, slavery and a serfdom that was little better than slavery prevented scientific advance and the kind of population explosion that might have created cost–push inflation all through the Middle Ages, the Renaissance and the Industrial Revolution, right down to the last two decades of the nineteenth century. Although the phenomenon of cost–push inflation clearly existed in these last years of the nineteenth century, its nature was not generally recognized until after World War I.

It is the theory of most businessmen and of some academic economists that the sole causes of creeping cost–push inflation are the demand for full employment and the workers' insistence on seeking to gain a bigger share in the gross national product too rapidly. This leads to the frequently heard charge that labor unions and politicians who give in to exorbitant demands by labor are responsible for cost–push inflation.

In this connection, we often hear businessmen, and even politicians, talk heatedly about keeping wage increases tied to increases in productivity, that labor should get only as much greater share of the GNP as can properly be attributed to workers' increase in hourly output of goods or services, either in physical volume or in the earning power of the enterprises for which they work.

In the sense that labor cannot seize something that does not exist, all labor of course must accept the self-evident fact that it cannot keep on enlarging its take unless the gross national product keeps on increasing. And within the competitive frame of reference of a given industry or business, labor cannot enlarge its share of the proceeds more rapidly than the competition will bear. To this extent, the businessmen and economists who want to tie wage increases to productivity gains make sense. But that is not the way most of them talk; rather, they talk as if tying wage increases to worker-productivity growth was a law taken right out of Holy Writ, something on a par with the Ten Commandments. To speak of the matter like that is to ignore all history and spout nonsense.

In the long run, wages cannot be tied continuously to productivity increases of the workers. The shoe is on the other foot. The workingman has struggled upward, as we have seen, from a slavery in which his employer held power of life and death over him and considered it unprofitable to keep him alive after about his thirty-fifth year. The memories of these wrongs of centuries, even millenniums, ago are not dead. Probably they never will die, but will continue forever to affect all dealings between employers and labor. Labor never will settle for long for anything less than taking another big bite out of the shares of capital owners and management in all productive enterprises.

Reasonably full employment was normal in the world until the Industrial Revolution. Serious unemployment occurred from time to time in all countries, but it was caused by the aftermath of war (war itself produced high employment), feudal aggression, famine and pestilence. Technological displacement of labor, bringing chronic unemployment, did not start until the invention of the spinning jenny and the power loom.

From that time on, all governments had to deal to some extent with unrest caused by chronic joblessness. The technological revolution still is accelerating, with consequent technological unemployment aggravated by racial prejudice, educational imbalance and other sociological factors. In many industries, technological displacement is temporary, affecting only one generation of workers. Certainly there are relatively more people in the textile and garment industries now than there were in the days of hand spinning and hand weaving, and workers in the modern highly mechanized printing trades comprise a much bigger proportion of the population than printing did in the days of hand-set type and hand-fed presses.

In fact, technology and automation have made manufacturing and the service industries, on the whole, employers of more workers than formerly, even though there are fewer workers engaged in actual production; they are employed in distribution, marketing, merchandising, finance, administration and in research and development to create new products.

On the other hand, in such basic industries as farming, lumbering, mining, fishing, seafaring and railroading, jobs and livelihoods of small proprietors have been wiped out by the millions and whole communities that depended on these jobs and small businesses have been ruined, with little or no hope of recovery.

Many political ideologies invented to deal with problems of social and economic justice generally have claimed they could eliminate chronic unemployment. The socialists said that if their motto, "From each according to his ability and to each according to his need," were followed faithfully, unemployment simply would vanish.

The communists adopted this slogan but added to it a cynical and brutal program of regimentation and oppression, to make it work by force. The fascists depended on a blend of supernationalist, emotional hypocrisy, drastic regimentation and economic and military aggression against other peoples to cure unemployment.

None of these ideologies has succeeded in averting chronic unemployment. The Soviet Union did manage to avoid any serious unemployment for almost half a century because the country was so backward at the time of the 1917 Revolution and had so far to travel in the effort to catch up with the Western world.

But very recently we have been hearing that in the past five years the Soviet Union has been hit by tremendous unemployment caused by rapid automation of Russian factories, growing mechanization of agriculture and a breakdown in the brutal discipline by which the masses were kept toiling for starvation wages by grim old Josef Stalin.

Stalin moved millions of Soviet citizens from their homelands in western and southern Russia to the icy steppes and forests of Siberia. His engineers and scientists built a large and successful industry in Siberia and the people he sent there did not dare leave their jobs and drift back home so long as Stalin lived and for some years after he died. But now, with more supportable regime in power at Moscow, it is reported that many of those sent to Siberia in Stalin's day are returning, and finding there is no work to be had in their old home regions.

From the start of the seventeenth century to the early 1920s, severe unemployment in Europe was relieved by mass emigration to the United States, but that became legally impossible after 1924. Chronic or intermittent serious unemployment thereafter afflicted many countries. Particularly hard-hit were Italy, Germany, Austria, several of the Balkan countries and Britain. France had unemployment, but along with such countries as Japan and Uruguay, turned very early to government policies designed to compel a high level of employment even at the sacrifice of technological progress. Unemployment was intermittent in the United States and Canada, and did not become severe until after the 1929 crash in Wall Street.

Most of the European countries tried government

measures to force full employment in the 1920s, but success was achieved only in France and there it was at the price of a continuing and humiliating inflation. Italy and Germany tried the fascist route, as did Japan eventually, and these disastrous adventures brought on World War II.

The United States did not attempt any substantial government moves to deal with unemployment until Franklin Roosevelt became President in 1933. The New Deal programs look far more successful in curbing unemployment in retrospect than they did at the time. Actually, they put more than half the army of unemployed to work rather quickly, but we still were left with a great many people out of work. During this period, Britain and Canada looked askance at the Roosevelt programs, considering them too expensive and visionary. Britain preferred the dole to "make-work" programs; apparently British politicians and economists believed that the only thing to do was to live as economically as possible, and sooner or later traditional economic forces would reassert themselves and restore prosperity.

That did not happen; it took a new world war to bring back prosperity.

The main story of commitment of all governments in the free world to a policy of achieving full employment at all costs thus does not start until after World War II. And the period in which we are most interested starts with stalemate in the Korean War in 1951. The years 1951–55 were an era of very stable prices in the United States in spite of steadily rising wages. But at the end of 1955, cost–push inflation made itself felt sharply and continued until the recession of 1958, when unemployment hit a new peak of 4.7 percent of the working force—more than 6.5 million people jobless—and prices started falling again. The 1958 recession was short-lived, and ever since 1959, even before our deep involvement in Vietnam began, we have had slow cost–push inflation.

During most of this period, farm prices and food prices have lagged behind rising industrial prices, a fact that makes the inflation supportable because inflated food prices naturally are the hardest to bear. The cost of services (except life insurance*) has gone up faster than the cost of commodities, and prices of manufactured commodities have gone up much faster than those of basic commodities, a fact that is the prime cause of economic distress in so many underdeveloped countries. Housing and other construction has gone up most rapidly of all.

Wages have increased in the United States in every year since 1933, and over the long pull they have gone up faster than prices. Output of workers per man-hour increased about 40 percent in the decade ending in 1957, and still is increasing, but more slowly. This increase in worker productivity in the decade ending in 1957 just about kept up with wage increases in real terms, i.e., the

---

* The cost of life insurance protection has been reduced substantially in the past several decades due to a vastly improved mortality experience, higher interest rates on life insurance investments and a reduction in the actual cost of doing business, for which the electronic computer is to a considerable extent responsible. For details, see my book *Life Insurance Stocks: An Investment Appraisal* (New York, Timely Publications, 1965).

physical amount of a specified list of basic goods and services that the wage dollar would buy. But dollar amounts of wages and the gross national product rose much faster than wages in real terms.

This difference between the rise in real wages, the rise in prices and the gross national product represents the amount of creeping cost–push inflation we have experienced—2 to 3 percent a year. Other advanced nations have had about the same experience we have. We have used the figures of this era only because they are complete and give us a little historical perspective. More up-to-date figures can be obtained from any financial magazine or from the federal government.

The experience of recent years shows clearly that whenever the unemployment rolls in the United States drop below 4 percent, the market for labor, both skilled and semiskilled, becomes tight in many industries.

This means that a large proportion, probably roughly half of the 4 percent who are jobless, are chronic unemployables for physical or psychological reasons. Some are unemployable because racial discrimination has plunged them into a frustrated refusal to try.

Of the other half, many are the so-called "frictionally unemployed," those whose jobs and livelihoods have been wiped out temporarily or permanently by the frictional strains of a constantly developing economy.

Sober economists say there is no doubt that the cost of supporting all these persons is more inflationary to the economy if we do it by heavy investments to put them to work in enterprises that do not produce immediate returns than if they are put on a dole. These economists make the further important point that frictional unemployment must be not merely tolerated, but wholeheartedly accepted. Industry cannot possibly progress and expand output to improve the standard of living unless managers have freedom to manage economically, and economical management is bound to produce frictional unemployment.

But even the more traditionalist of the economists concede that the social, political and moral cost of keeping two to three million Americans in stultifying idleness on a dole is in the long run greater and more dangerous to the fabric of American society than that of trying to create useful jobs for as many of them as we can, even if their work does not earn a profit for anyone.

In other words, all Americans are firmly committed to accept inflation to provide jobs.

7.

DEFLATION:
NO PANACEA

For centuries the sole method of dealing with inflation was to slash wages brutally and lay off workers in swarms. This choked off the supply of money and the demand for goods; prices had to come down and the air was squeezed out of the economy. This method was tried in the Great Depression that started in 1929, but it did not work.

It always had worked in the past, though. That the workers went hungry, and that their women and children actually died of starvation, did not matter. There were plenty of clodhopper peasants in all countries, and the jungles of Africa teemed with savages who could be hunted down and imported as slaves if labor really got scarce.

Naturally, this kept the wage level very low. Ancient and medieval literature contains some interesting tracts on the art of feeding slaves and serfs just sufficiently to keep them alive and to keep them from living so long as to be a burden on their masters after their useful years were over.

As late as the eighteenth century, it was accepted that the natural wage of labor of all kinds was just enough to keep body and soul together. The three most prominent early economists, Adam Smith, David Ricardo and Robert Malthus, all propounded this idea as a "law of wages." If wages were allowed to rise above the subsistence level, the laboring classes would breed too rapidly and labor would become too plentiful. Unemployment would result, forcing wages down. If wages sank too low, workers would starve to death and the resulting scarcity would force wages up. Apparently, it never occurred to the nobility, the mercantile classes or the churches that this brutal situation could or should be changed.

Even Karl Marx accepted the subsistence theory of the natural price of labor, but Marx added something extremely important to the law of wages—the Surplus Value theory. Writing in the mid-nineteenth century, *after* the Industrial Revolution already had widely introduced labor-saving machinery, Marx wrote that the laborer still was paid for a day's work a price about equal to his subsistence cost, but that he was compelled by society to work longer hours and produce much more in goods and services than the amount that actually would buy his and his family's bare subsistence. This surplus value, Marx said, was taken from the laborer by his employer without compensation.

Marx was proved absolutely correct as time went on. Traditional economists were forced to accept his theory of Surplus Value. No economic system can operate without a surplus value of labor.

A mechanic in a good garage today is paid perhaps $4.50 an hour, but the customer is billed for his services at $8 to $10 an hour. The difference between that and $4.50 is surplus value, and the whole struggle between employer and union is over the worker's struggle to recapture more of this surplus value. Every big company's cost accountants have clear ideas of what is the surplus value of the various kinds of labor they employ.

Ironically, probably the highest surplus values of labor in the modern world, and those in which the workers often share the least, prevail in the Communist countries where Marx is worshipped as a saint. It seems likely that Marx would be highly indignant at the wage policies pursued by the governments in many of the so-called Marxist countries.

In our time, the subsistence theory of the natural price of labor has had to be abandoned entirely, because of the rise of collective bargaining. Instead, we operate on the theory that there is no natural price of labor but that the price is determined by the relative bargaining power of worker and employer, which obviously can be affected by many factors.

The historical trend of wage levels in the United States proves that bargaining power is the determining factor. There are no records of wage trends in colonial America for the simple reason that there were no wage earners. All menials then either were slaves or indentured servants. Free people were farmers, tradesmen or hunters and trappers, small capitalists. Nor are there any reliable figures on wage trends in the Republic until about 1840.

But between 1840 and 1890, wages in the United States at least doubled in real terms. And economist Paul H. Douglas, the former Democratic senator from Illinois, has shown that hourly manufacturing wages in real terms rose an average of 44 percent between 1890 and 1926. Between 1929 and 1933, hourly factory wages dropped from 52.2 to 43.7 cents, an extremely sharp fall.

Thereafter, unionization expanded rapidly and labor's bargaining power increased. Wages rose steadily, slowly at first, and then at an accelerating pace until hourly factory wages averaged $2.61 in 1965. However, the 1965 figure is in money terms, not real terms.

Wage slashes and layoffs were quite successful in ending the periodic panics of the nineteenth century in the United States, including regional panics accompanied by greenback inflation. There were a number of these money panics. The two most severe were those of 1857 and 1873. They were not accompanied by classic inflation, but rather were the result of stock jobbing, unbridled speculation and some very injudicious railway and industrial expansion. The 1857 panic followed a spectacular wave of railroad building, some of it into territory that would not provide nearly enough business to support the new railways for some years yet. The financing of these ventures included an awful lot of watered stock, much of which was sold to English and continental European investors. When the infant railroads inevitably went bankrupt and were reorganized, the European investors and many creditors were frozen out. Then, in the 1850s, interest rates in Europe went up so that European capital suddenly withdrew from Wall Street. As a result, American banks went down like tenpins, 1,400 in a single month. Unemployment was widespread. Wages were slashed mercilessly. But the situation improved quite rapidly and when the Civil War began four years later, the country was fairly prosperous.

The panic of 1873 is also generally attributed to stock jobbing and reckless speculation and to the failure of President Grant's administration to keep the pirates and rascals of Wall Street in check. Again wage slashes squeezed the air out of the economy, but this time there was no swift recovery in spite of the fact that the nation's economy was expanding and the western lands inhabited by the Indians were being opened up to settlement. For the next twenty years, the general price and wage movement was barely sideways and in some years the trend definitely was downward. But from the early 1890s to the end of World War I, things really moved ahead. This era experienced possibly the fastest economic growth, in real terms, the world had seen anywhere.

Americans believed their economy was growing at a very fast rate in the 1920s. The urban centers of the land grew like mushrooms, with skyscrapers sprouting even in the prairie cities. Thousands and thousands of miles of new concrete highways were built. The automotive industry became a giant and newer basic industries, such as petroleum, rubber and aluminum, built huge installations. The motion picture film and theater business, radio broadcasting and the infant electronics industry grew very fast. The beginning of a substantial airline and aircraft industry developed. The pace of technological progress was very rapid.

But there was a dangerous lopsidedness about this growth. Production and productive capacity were growing much faster than consumption or ability to consume. The ending of free immigration from Europe in 1924 caused a fairly serious drop in the rate of family formation. The birth rate had leveled off somewhat. The holding in a state of near-peonage of the large Negro minority kept a very substantial number of Americans from being good consumers.

Foreign markets were almost totally neglected and it was the fashion to boast about how self-contained the American economy was. Few American manufacturers wanted to be bothered about exports. We were turning out huge annual surpluses of farm products, including food and cotton, but we could not sell these abroad because neither business nor the Coolidge administration would bother to establish any export credit system or work out any bilateral trade arrangements with consuming countries. The Republican Party considered the profits of high-cost American manufacturers much more sacred than the welfare of the American farmer, whose ability to consume was rapidly being undermined by the malaise of the primary farm product markets. There were constant revolt and threat of revolt by the farm bloc in the Republican Party.

But the most serious lopsidedness in the economy was in wages; they were low and tended to fall lower as the 1920s advanced. The American workingman had the highest standard of living in the world, and that standard was rising because accelerating production reduced prices of many kinds of goods. But wages and salaries, as we can see now in retrospect, were very low in relation to the productive capacity of the economy. This was reflected in the great difficulties experienced in the 1920s in expanding consumer credit. The automobile finance companies expanded installment credit quite successfully, but banks, loan companies and other industries found it hard to increase the volume of consumer finance loans except at high cost and big losses. The wage level simply did not give the worker enough margin over the subsistence level to meet substantial monthly installments as it does today.

This was not perceived at the time or at least it was very ill-perceived for the simple reason that, for the most part, American affairs were run by very ignorant, opinionated men. The practice or knowledge of rational economic principles was virtually nonexistent in business and government. Indeed, most economics teaching in the colleges in the 1920s was abysmal, based on ideas already fifty years out of date. Economics professors were commonly third-rate scholars suspected of being pretty much dilettantes by their colleagues in the classical humanities and hard scientific disciplines.

The general climate of the Government and business world was violently anti-intellectual and militantly unscientific. Typically, during most of the 1920s, the dawn of the age of aviation, we had a President in the White House who hated airplanes and was widely reputed to consider the whole idea of man flying to be presumptuous, ostentatious and possibly immoral. Today, nobody could say whether Cal Coolidge really had such ideas because during all his years in the White House cautious Cal never committed himself in public about anything. Like Charles II, Coolidge "never said a foolish thing nor ever did a wise one."

In the last year of Coolidge's administration and the first six months of Herbert Hoover's term in the White House, the most reckless stock market speculation in modern American history occurred—the Great Bull Market that brought on the crash of October 24, 1929, and the resulting financial panic. In the next few months, the classic medicine for dealing with panics—extreme credit stringency, wage cuts and layoffs of workers—was applied with vigor. But instead of having a curative effect, the medicine made things a great deal worse. Banks and businesses kept on failing by the thousands. Hundreds of thousands of people lost their homes and farms and mortgages were foreclosed.

A look at the actual percentage declines that occurred in economic statistics from peak to trough in the 1929–1933 depression is enough to make one shudder. It seems barely believable that it all could have happened. The gross national product, expressed in constant dollars, fell by 28.4 percent, output of durable goods dropped 73.5 percent and overall industrial output by 49.4 percent, while personal income fell 49.7 percent and retail sales by 43.5 percent. Nonfarm employment dropped 30.7 percent—almost one worker in three out of a job. Nobody ever got around to counting the people without work on the farms. Corporate profits fell by 135.6 percent.

And all this occurred on a drop in the price level of only 26.5 percent. Wage cuts averaged 28 percent.

In spite of the terrible way things were going, it looked briefly in 1931 as if recovery might be "just around the corner," as Mr. Hoover assured the public it was. But in that year, the crash struck Britain, France and Germany simultaneously and hit them even harder than it hit the United States. The establishments of all three countries defaulted on big financial obligations to the United States, thus severely aggravating the tight-money situation on this side of the Atlantic and sending the American economy into a new tailspin.

Why did the classic medicine fail? Nobody seemed to understand why at the time, but in retrospect the answer seems pretty clear. The business community, President Hoover, and state and local governments failed to distinguish between the money panic caused by the stock market gambling and the strains created by the structural weaknesses in the real basic economy; most particularly, they failed to comprehend how severely depressed wages and salaries were in relation to output potential and the inadequacies of consumer credit. There also were many structural weaknesses in corporate financial setups and marketing arrangements, caused mainly by the lack of genuine economic knowledge and consequent widespread naïveté of the business and banking communities and the public officials.

As a result, the moves taken to deal with the financial panic—wage cuts, layoffs, tax slashes and severe restrictions on credit—simply turned out to be sledge hammer blows against the weaker points in the underpinning of the basic economy. The underconsumption was exacerbated to fantastic proportions. Naturally, things kept getting worse.

When Franklin Delano Roosevelt became President in 1933, things were made critical by a severe crisis in public confidence. The four years of extremely tight economy under Hoover had not strengthened the federal government's credit or made money easier. On the contrary, money and credit virtually had vanished from the land.

Roosevelt took about the only course open to him. He halved the gold content of the dollar in order to get collateral for new Government financing, then proceeded to launch as many programs as he and his New Deal advisers could think of to get people to working and consuming—to prime the pump and get wages and prices to moving upward instead of downward. The progress was slow even though FDR aroused considerable initial enthusiasm; he also aroused the undying hatred of the predatory and reactionary elements in the population who, considering how badly they had mismanaged things in the previous twelve years, were lucky to have escaped being liquidated in a revolution.

But this was the last time widespread wage cuts were tried by industry and commerce as a means of dealing with a financial panic and its aftermath. Since 1930 industry has been as opposed to wage cuts as the unions as a general rule. It is now generally accepted that, as a cure, drastic deflation is likely to prove worse than the disease.

8.

THE
SCARCITY MYTH

The classic description of inflation is that it is the upward pressure on prices caused by an over-supply of money and extreme scarcity of goods. Indeed, from very ancient times all monetary theory and law has been based on the omnipresence in the world of scarcity of the real things men need to survive.

But modern cost–push inflation rarely results from scarcity because there is very little classic scarcity in the modern world. In most countries, such scarcity as we have results from faulty management and from slavishly following financial and political policies that rest on out-dated premises. Of course, there are war-torn areas and backward regions where scarcity still is real, and the whole world does have long-term problems about food and basic commodities. But most economists believe that classic scarcity is not likely to return soon in the Western world or in the Soviet Union unless there is another major war.

This fact makes mincemeat of much economic theory that has been accepted as gospel for a long time. It weakens the foundations of a social and moral philosophy that constant thrift is required to combat universal scarcity. It casts doubt also on the sincerity of conventional protestations of economists and businessmen that they believe in free competition.

Inflation is a phenomenon of money, but money is not real. At least it is not real in the sense that things we can eat, wear or otherwise use functionally are real. Money is totally dependent for its value on what people think about it. This is true whether we are talking about hard money such as gold, or paper notes backed by gold or silver, or about the many other kinds of money that are created by the capitalization of credit, debt or earning power. In fact, in the world economy as it operates today, the biggest and most important money exists only as bookkeeping entries or in such paper symbols as notes, stocks and bonds—and all of these things are only capitalized debt or credit. But, as John Law found out, credit, which is another name for debt, is highly expansible. As I often caution my friends, there are about two hundred real dollars in the world. All the rest is bookkeeping.

For example, the stock of a corporation having thirty million shares outstanding in the hands of knowledgeable business investors goes up one dollar a share on the exchange. Instantly and automatically bookkeeping entries totaling $30 million in new paper value are created for the owners of the outstanding shares.

This paper value of $30 million can serve as collateral for perhaps another $25 million in credit, loans that become new bookkeeping entries for other paper owners, who may in turn borrow against them. And the new lenders can borrow in turn. Soon, although no gold or silver, land, food or other real commodities have changed hands, the one dollar share rise in a single company's stock may inflate the nation's total supply of credit money temporarily by close to $100 million.

Considering the frequent rapid rises of stocks on the average and considering that 2,500 companies are listed on the two biggest exchanges in the United States along with thousands of other big companies having large amounts of stock traded over the counter, the stock market alone can inflate and deflate the overall money supply very rapidly.

Add to that the bond market and the hundreds of millions of dollars of funding transactions of various other kinds executed in business every day, and you begin to realize that the currency may actually be a small factor in the overall problem of inflation. This credit-and-debt inflation is vastly greater in magnitude than the cost–push inflation created by deliberate policies designed to provide continuing full employment.

Competition is supposed to curb inflation or even to prevent it, but as John K. Galbraith* and David T. Bazelon† have observed, businessmen do not really mean

---

* *In Defense of Business: A Strategic Appraisal*, (Cambridge, Mass., Harvard University Press, 1961).
† *The Paper Economy* (New York, Random House, 1959–1964).

free and unrestricted production and marketing of goods and services when they speak of competition. They are talking about what Bazelon calls "balance sheet competition" and that, he says ironically, leads to very strenuous noncompetition; that is, reducing inventories to create artificial scarcity so prices may be raised, thus creating inflation.

That appears to make nonsense of the preachments of conservative academic economists, chambers of commerce and tub-thumping politicians who proclaim that the free market is self-coordinating and self-regulating. In fact, the tendency to avoid free competition by almost any conceivable means while praising its virtues is perhaps the most notable characteristic of modern business. That is why our Government employs such a big army of antitrust lawyers.

A few years ago, there was a great hue and cry in Washington and in the financial press about "administered prices"; that is, prices for goods and services fixed by business on the basis of cost factors, desired profit levels and amortization of development and marketing investments without the intervention of direct competition in the market place.

One might have imagined from the tone of the rumblings that administered prices were something new in the world. The truth is, prices always have been administered and always there has been a terrific conflict between the operation of the so-called law of supply and demand and the usually successful efforts of producers and merchants to dispense with considerations of supply and demand and operate their businesses on a much safer and more profitable basis. Supply and demand was all right for peasants and laborers, who were allowed to starve by the thousands when their crops and their skills became too plentiful; in time of scarcity, they might be tossed a bone in the shape of slightly better prices or wages, but the peasants still were just as likely to starve by reason of having little to sell, and the workers to go hungry for want of employment.

In ancient societies and, indeed, down through Tudor times in England, retail prices and wages were administered with a brutal frankness and with no regard for supply and demand. The whole system was designed for centuries to protect the rich and keep the masses down. Labor either was enslaved or, if nominally free, kept in subjection by *maximum*, not minimum, wage laws. It was a serious criminal offense to pay a laborer a penny more than the officially administered wage scale.

On the other hand, officially administered prices, as often as not, were minimum at the retail level, but uncontrolled at wholesale. Prices went up in time of scarcity, but they were not allowed to go down for the consumer no matter how plentiful things got. A baker could be flogged, jailed or mutilated for selling a loaf of bread to a hungry man for a farthing less than the official price, but a rich merchant trading at wholesale could charge all the traffic would bear or dump merchandising as cheaply as he pleased to other dealers.

It is no wonder that Adam Smith,‡ the father of economics, wrote bluntly that "the purpose of all government is to defend the rich from the poor."

So, in the past, administered prices and wages assured the rich, who included the aristocracy descended from the warrior class, of a monopoly on wealth and power with no threats from the vagaries of the marketplace. But since the Renaissance and the opening of the oceans in the sixteenth century to world trade, we have had a marketplace so wide it could not be ignored. Something had to be added to the medieval system of vassalage to take the place of rigidly administered prices and wages, in order to preserve the power and privilege of the wealthy.

That something is called profit.

The distinctive thing about profit is that it is something that the owner of a business considers himself entitled to over and above compensation for his services. It is actually a pretty new idea in the world. In the past, businessmen talked of gains—that amount they got for something exceeding what they paid for it, and the gains included all compensation for the businessman's personal services and for the use of his money, his warehouse or other facilities.

One eminent economist, Professor Frank H. Knight, has written: "In the Idealized society of the equilibrium theory, there would be no occasion for assigning the distinctive name of profit to any type of return."

---

‡ Adam Smith: eighteenth-century English economist.

In other words, says Professor Knight, if the free marketplace really were self-coordinating and self-regulating, there could be no room for profit. Money and other capital could not be allowed to earn any return other than fixed interest charges. The capitalists who served in the management of a commercial or a productive enterprise would be entitled to substantial wages, but those who put in only money, no toil or skill, could receive only interest.

Of course, not many economists or businessmen will agree with Professor Knight's narrow definition of profit. They will insist that profit is also substantial sums which the businessman returns to his business or to other businesses to create new jobs and new wealth for society. Therefore, profit is essential even in a self-regulating economy.

Profit probably is the most important single source of inflation in the modern world. Business has learned how to turn nearly all profits into capitalized credit or debt and thus inflate the overall supply of money paper many times. Even the currency itself can be inflated in this matter as commercial banks draw ever larger supplies of currency from central banks to meet the demand created by the conversion of profits into capitalized debt and credit.

Before I have my readers jumping to the conclusion that I regard inflation resulting from profits as a nightmarish evil that will engulf us all and destroy our money, let me hasten to say I am *not* against profit and I do not think the inflation of the overall money supply produced by capitalizing profit and using it as collateral for debt need necessarily have any deleterious impact on ordinary people. It does inflate prices. Prices have to go up periodically to keep the whole structure of capitalized debt and profit from collapsing. But wages also go up, often faster than prices.

So, today we have an economic system which, instead of obeying laws observed by Adam Smith or Karl Marx and supposedly based on automatic, inexorable social or market mechanisms, actually is administered by several layers of bureaucrats. The interests and purposes of these bureaucrats sometimes mesh admirably for the common good, but just as frequently they clash savagely. Most powerful is the managerial bureaucracy. It has taken over from the old rugged individualists, capitalists and aristocrats who ran their own enterprises. As Bazelon notes, the managerial bureaucracy has been left "ideologically naked" by the collapse of conventional economic theory. But that only compels the corporate managers to resort to a lot of rather shabby public relations techniques; it does not deprive them of their ability, which is grounded in part on genuine technological and psychological skill and in part on greed and plain power politics. Not only does the managerial bureaucracy administer prices, but it also administers wages, allocates resources and creates and maintains markets.

The scientists and engineers are another layer of bureaucrats involved deeply in the workings of the economic system. Politicians, Government officials and lawyers form a third layer of bureaucrats of growing importance. Finally, the most clamorous layer at present is the union bureaucracy but its might derives mainly from its ability to exert the pressure of the workers' voting power on the politicians and Government bureaucrats.

Observe that the nominal owners of our modern economic system, the stockholders, usually wield the least power and have the least to say of anybody about the operation of business. This is true even when substantial stock holdings are concentrated in large and powerful institutions, such as big insurance companies and mutual funds. Why is this? It is because from the point of view of the economist, ownership has become so fragmented and depersonalized as to be almost devoid of meaning. Of course, there are exceptions. A considerable number of fairly large companies still are family owned and controlled, but the number is diminishing and those that survive tend to find that they are just as subject to the layers of bureaucratic control as General Motors or A. T. & T.

So, today's society is composed of people who have the use of more goods and services than any generation of the past dreamed was possible—yet they own practically nothing.

You have a title to a car, but the finance company's claim is better at law than yours. The same goes for your mortgaged house, the appliances you have bought on installments and the stocks you hold on margin. If you run your own business, the interest in it of the bank, the suppliers and other creditors, and even the vested interest in their jobs your employees claim through their unions, may make your equity seem pretty scant. And the Government puts some pretty sharp limitations on how you can run the business.

In short, in the modern world, ownership of anything has a large element of illusion about it.

This is not a new idea. Thorstein Veblen, probably the greatest American economist, wrote an article back in 1898 implying that man originally derived the notion of private property when a primal savage clubbed a female into submission in the forest, carried her off and sequestered her for his exclusive enjoyment.

But Veblen went on to imply that the poor savage deluded himself, because instead of owning the woman he soon was compelled to suspect that she owned him. Personally, I suspect it actually was the woman who first thought of the permanent and exclusive arrangement. She was tired of being slugged and possessed by a succession of plug-uglies she had never seen before.

9.

INFLATION
OR PROGRESS?

The chief beneficiaries of long-term inflation in the United States are those who scream the loudest about the horrors of inflation. They are the so-called vested interests. They include bankers, big insurance companies, the big Government financial agencies, the mutual funds, the rich universities and foundations, the wealthier churches, the industrial and mercantile corporations and our growing army of millionaires. Did you know that there are one hundred thousand millionaires in the country now, and the number is believed to be growing by five thousand a year?

It is these people and these institutions who are able to make use of capitalized business debt and earnings and even of the capitalized consumer debt of seventy-odd million workers as collateral to create ever new mountains of debt capital.

Why should these people be so concerned about inflation if they benefit from it? The answer lies in the darker recesses of the human psyche, and in the long history of the struggle between the haves and have-nots of the world.

In fact, some people's fear of inflation is really a fear of the masses and a fear of an overabundance of goods. In modern terms, they are psychologically afraid of abundance for the same reason that the barons and wealthy merchants of medieval Europe were afraid of the prosperity created by seigniorage. They are afraid that by raising the poor to their level in terms of worldly goods, abundance will deprive them of the superior privileges and status they now enjoy.

These feelings were held consciously and were freely expressed in former times by the aristocrats and privileged classes. Today, they seldom are put into words, because they would be so unpopular that even those who have such feelings could not express them out loud, and continue to live with their own consciences. But the fact that these feelings have been pushed back from verbalized thought into the emotional sphere does not make them any less real or psychologically potent.

The relationship between price inflation as opposed to continuously expanded production and these deep-rooted psychological fears is clear, but rather intricate. For example, until about 1940, the labor unions did not become powerful enough in the United States to exercise any significant upward pressure on the price level, but long before then the so-called vested interests pushed prices up periodically and had succeeded in wiping out nearly every vestige of genuine price competition in the American economy.

Back in the 1920s and 1930s, higher prices generally were described as "progress," not as inflation. Did not higher prices create more jobs, more investments in plant, more profits, more purchasing power and the accumulation of capital and savings? Of course they did. Not infrequently, businessmen still speak of higher prices as progress. Price boosts are eagerly sought whenever management thinks the traffic will bear them. Yet, if prices go up without any clearly visible increase in the physical demand for the goods and services in question, then, by definition, money is being inflated. And that is what has been happening in the United States, or at least prices have been going up faster than the visible demand for goods. In some products, notably automobiles, prices have gone up in the face of a visible and substantial decline in demand.

The big motivation for inflationary price increases is not hard to find. It is the almost universal American desire for the fast buck—to make money in ever increasing amounts without going to the trouble to produce and market better goods and services. Some businessmen find it easier and less risky to make big profits by systematically and periodically inflating the price level. Similarly, labor seeks to get bigger prices for its services and sometimes even to collect for services not rendered by means of featherbedding rules in union contracts, and by many other devices.

This does not mean that genuine technological, industrial and merchandising progress is thereby prevented. On the contrary, our economy makes enormous genuine progress in spite of price and wage inflation, perhaps even because of it in some degree.

But suppose the vested interests and the fast-buck boys were forced by a tough government to embark on seeking profits solely by producing and distributing more and better goods and services and selling them without resorting to periodic price inflation. Then what would happen?

We know what would transpire because this has happened twice in comparatively recent years, during World War II and during the Korean War. In both eras production went up astronomically and there was some price inflation, but the inflation was held in check by direct Government controls. When the wars ended, some deflation set in as demand subsided. But the deflation was short-lived. The debt-capitalization game soon was resumed and slow but steady price inflation began. The price raises were very slow though; in fact, the years between 1960 and 1965 almost could be called years of price stability.

So we can conclude that scarcity, like excess, is artificial in modern society—and is caused by war or manipulation to create excessive profits.

This raises the suspicion that if we really could get free competition in the production of goods and services obedient to demand, everybody soon would have practically all of everything he could consume. That certainly would eliminate any excuse for inflation.

But if the economy produced so much that everybody could have as much of everything as he could consume and he could be reasonably sure that his children would enjoy the same felicitous circumstances, what use would a man have for idle wealth, or wealth to produce profits? What real reason would he have for wanting to leave his children an estate? Of course, he still would want to leave his widow provided for, but the national economy could be safely depended on to care for the kids abundantly so long as they stayed out of jail, weren't halfwits or weren't too lazy to work a minimum number of hours a day. In such a society, a man who insisted on getting rich would look more than a little silly. The socialists and the technocrats have been insisting for a long time that such a society ultimately is possible. But the traditional economists cling to the economics of scarcity. They believe that neither the known resources of our planet nor the intellectual and emotional capacities of human beings in the aggregate will support any such optimistic view.

A lot of people who identify their personal interests with those of the vested interests become terribly frightened at the merest suspicion that there might be a glimmer of truth in the abundance theories of the socialists and technocrats. They realize only too well that if such an economic millennium ever came about, the power that wealth and property have wielded in the world ever since the days of the cavemen will come to an end. That prospect cannot be faced by the lords of money, business and government. It can only be faced by historians, some economists and other scholars and by hordes of salaried workers.

But it is the salaried workers who hold the votes.

So the people who have the money power and the political power and many who wield academic power cling to their faith in the economics of scarcity even though scarcity is no more real in the peacetime world today than demons and witches. Some of them continue to busy themselves feverishly making profits by inflating the price level and keeping the brakes on the production of goods and services. Thereby they protect the vast mountains of capitalized debt money built up since the 1929 market crash.

I believe Veblen was the first economist to comment seriously on the then new phenomenon of capitalizing assets on the basis of their earning power rather than on their intrinsic or functional value. So I doubt if Veblen would be surprised by the fact that today we also capitalize—and inflate—the purchasing power of workers. It is an observable irony of our economic system that as the ordinary citizen becomes less useful to business as a worker because of automation and technological progress, he becomes more valuable as a consumer. It pays to pay him inflated wages for doing less work because he can contribute so much more to the profits of business by spending than by working. The hundred and fifty dollars or so he pays out monthly on his car and other installment purchases is inflated a number of times as capitalized and recapitalized debt that earns paper profits.

But why doesn't the whole structure just collapse periodically if there is so much air in it? Why don't we have more violent deflationary upheavals and sudden money panics?

The answer is pretty clear. Note that I included Government financial agencies among the vested interests. Indeed, the Government fast is becoming the biggest vested interest and it too earns paper profits on capitalized debt and collects large amounts in income taxes on the paper profits business makes out of capitalized debt. So, ever since 1933 in the United States, and much earlier in some countries, government has underwritten the whole game so heavily that in large, strong countries like the United States, the Soviet Union, Britain and France, it appears that violent money upheavals no longer are possible except when war brings general catastrophe.

Of course, not all economists or business experts accept this last conclusion. Many think we could have another 1929 disaster, perhaps rather suddenly, particularly if as individuals we become too self-centered and refuse to face up to the need for restraint and sacrifice for the common good.

In any case, even if creeping inflation by means of capitalized debt and earning power is profitable to the moneyed classes and highly tolerable to salary and wage earners, it still bears harshly on pensioners, annuitants, many institutional employees and others who either must live on fixed incomes or whose salary bargaining power is excessively weak. It is not capitalized debt profit that harms these persons, only the price inflation that may result.

That poses the big question of what to do about these inequities, since obviously no one nowdays wants to go back to violent periodic deflation as a corrective. That medicine simply is too harsh.

An increasing number of economists and sociologists contend that the problem will be solved only when the matter finally is taken out of the hands of the vested interests by dealing a *coup de grâce* to the whole theory and practice of the economics of scarcity. Two methods of accomplishing this are proposed: direct Government price controls or strong intervention by the Government to step up production and distribution of goods and services.

In the first case, direct Government controls, prices would have to stop rising, and business could only hope for new profits out of increased volume, probably at smaller margins and greater efficiency. In the second case, forced draft production, prices simply would have to go down and consumption up, and again business would be totally dependent on increased efficiency for profitability.

Neither idea is palatable to many businessmen or to those nonproductive shareholders whom Veblen contemptuously labeled the leisure class. But even if you put them all together, businessmen and the leisure class can muster very few votes compared to the army of salaried workers. Add in the pensioners, particularly the

Social Security pensioners, the annuitants and the others who feel themselves squeezed by price inflation—these people already are doing a slow burn, and are becoming increasingly aware of their potential political power—then ultimately the votes will be available to compel Government intervention to wipe out subservience to the economics of scarcity and insist on continuous expansion of production.

We need not be terrified at the long-range prospect of such a drastic change, because before it came about, many things would have occurred to soften its impact. For one thing, a rather high proportion of the individuals who make up the moneyed classes and control the interlocking, but loose, conglomeration of capital and power, which I have called the vested interests, would have seen the light and taken steps to bring about change. Some very prominent business leaders, particularly some of those with a scientific or engineering background, already have caught a vision of the future and are trying to lead their colleagues out of the wilderness of traditional scarcity economics.

For example, Dr. Simon Ramo, the scientist-financier who created TRW, Incorporated, and the Bunker Ramo Corporation, wrote an article entitled *Toward a Trillion Dollar GNP.** Dr. Ramo is a free-enterpriser all the way, but he is first of all a scientist and a humanitarian. His article had almost nothing to say about profits. Instead, Dr. Ramo talked of expanding production and the

---

* *Finance Magazine*, February, 1968.

distribution of goods and services without limit to solve the social problems of our age, which he labeled the Awkward Age. He wants to use the electronic computer and other scientific marvels not only to expand output of goods rapidly, but to build new highways, plan and carry out crash programs to combat air and water pollution, deal with the overconcentration of population in crowded cities, halt waste of natural resources and to step up the expansion and improvement of all educational and medical facilities. He wrote that businessmen have been too busy piping TV dinners and Teflon pans into homes, "but we have not thought in terms of applying technology to society's large unfilled wants."

We could use more Simon Ramos.

10.

AN OUNCE OF
PREVENTION...

An ounce of prevention is worth a pound of cure."

Insofar as runaway inflation is concerned, the old saw is doubly true. It is much easier to prevent inflation from getting out of hand than to restore the situation once it happens. Even if the situation is restored, the losses and hardships runaway inflation causes leave their scars— they are never retrieved.

The duty to provide the ounce of prevention rests on each and every one of us individually.

In fact, the ordinary citizen alone has the power to prevent inflation. He alone has the proper objectivity and proper incentives to do the job. As we have seen, business and industry have a vested interest in continued inflation. Business and industry suffer the least from inflation when it does get out of hand. Indeed, businessmen and industrialists often are able to profit quite handsomely from runaway inflation.

Therefore, it is very foolish of the ordinary citizen to look to the leaders of the business community to protect him from dangerous inflation.

The whole history of our country shows this to be true. Most of our early money panics were caused by speculative fever, and speculative fever resulted largely from the irresponsible greed of the businessman chasing the fast buck—not from the spending habits of ordinary persons. The businessman and the industrialist do not set out to cause inflation. They simply become so absorbed in chasing profits that, even though they believe their activities are wholly in the public interest because they are "creating prosperity," they may actually be behaving irresponsibly. In particular, they may be engaging in pricing policies that are strongly inflationary. They acquire a *deformation professionelle* which deludes them into thinking that anything that increases the paper profitability of their little sector of the economy has to be in the general public interest, which may not be true at all. Inflation results and eventually panic may result.

The most striking demonstration of this occurred in the 1920s, when businessmen and industrialists pushed their manufacturing and trading profits and especially their paper speculative profits in the stock market sky-high and paid no attention to the manner in which the farming population and the working class, both blue collar and white collar, were being left behind and were not sharing adequately in the rewards of economic progress.

Nor can we, as ordinary citizens, depend on our public

officials and politicians to protect us from runaway
inflation. We subject our public officials and politicians
to far too many special interest and group pressures to
enable them to maintain complete objectivity about finances and economics. A congressman whose constituents are dependent, or believe themselves to be dependent, for their continued happiness on maintaining
an artificially high price of whatumacallits manufactured
in the district, simply cannot refuse to go along with his
constituents even though keeping the price of whatumacallits up can be shown to have an inflationary effect
on the general economy. Every public official and politician is subject to one or more such special pressures,
which are not really in the public interest and may well
be inflationary in their long-range impact.

Quite aside from that, as citizens of the first democratic republic created in the modern world, we Americans believe, as the cardinal tenet of our national philosophy, that ultimate responsibility for everything rests
on the common citizen, not on officials, politicians, gen-
erals or the vested propertied interests. We believe all
power similarly rests in the common man, not in money
or bureaucracy.

If we stop believing that, and stop accepting our ultimate responsibility as individual citizens for our national
policies in our daily lives, then we might as well turn
the country over to the technocrats, the socialists, the
communists or a fascist party that will be only too glad
to assume all the responsibility, all the power, and pro-

ceed to regiment us and order us around like a nation of 200 million sheep.

If we abdicate our responsibilities as citizens to the politicians and to the business and financial community, the task of sensible economic management then will become much more difficult. Although, a hundred years ago, it was fashionable even among scholars to contend that government by an aristocracy or a powerful elite was more likely to be enlightened and efficient than government by the democratic mob, all history proves the exact opposite to be true. Very little social or technological progress ever was made under feudal governments. Democratic regimes, whether based on free-enterprise economics or socialist economics, have produced vastly more progress. It is hard for Americans to think of communism as a variety of democracy, since all power in a Communist nation rests in the party bureaucracy. Yet Communism has been remarkably successful in employing the most important democratic tenet: The citizens of the Communist countries, in general, have been successfully inspired to accept and take seriously the civic and social responsibilities communist philosophy imposes on them as individuals. The zeal and dedication of the mass of the population in Communist countries never ceases to astonish trained Western observers.

But in spite of obtaining the zealous support of a large proportion of their populaces, Communist regimes invariably distrust the masses more than free-enterprise democratic regimes and rule by harsh, rigid and tyrannical methods that frustrate the energies of the people to a substantial degree.

And that brings us right down to precisely what we can do as individuals to prevent inflation, to halt in its tracks the creeping inflation presently going on in the United States.

The most important step is to adopt a conscientious and industrious attitude toward your job or your business. The biggest cause of creeping inflation is plain goldbricking.

If there were no goldbricking by workers of all grades, including supervisors and executives, in the automobile industry alone, that car that has to sell for $3,500 could sell for $3,000; the painting job on your home that costs $1,200 would cost only $900 if the workers gave the boss a full day's work for a full day's wage, and if the boss painter did not tack an extra $100 onto the bill.

Look around you in the factory, store or office where you work. How many of your fellow workers really give the company full time or the full effort the job calls for? Precious few. . . . The whole idea in American offices, shops and factories today is "Take it easy, Pal!" This attitude on the part of nearly all of us actually may be a greater inflationary influence on the American economy than the war in Vietnam.

Greed on the part of businessmen is just as reprehensible in causing inflation. The newspapers are filled with accounts of complaints to the Better Business Bureaus regarding sharp practices and padded bills sent to customers by all sorts of merchandising and service companies—the automatic transmission repair shop that makes a routine practice of running up a bill of around $200 for a job that really is not needed at all; the big pharmaceutical houses that still charge markups of 500 to 700 percent on branded drugs, the development costs of which were recouped years ago; the retail stores in ghetto neighborhoods that mark up prices on foods and the other necessities substantially more than do their counterparts in better neighborhoods; ghetto landlords who gouge poor minorities shamelessly for vermin-infested, ill-heated, crowded filthy tenement flats. Finally, what about the many businessmen, even including some merchants and bankers who are supposed to be eminently respectable, who shamelessly pad installment finance charges with phony items, and then take advantage of the holder-in-due-course doctrine of our credit laws to legalize the swindles? All these practices also contribute mightily to unnecessary creeping inflation, inflation that is not buying social progress.

Let's get back for a minute to that matter of a full day's work for a full day's wage. For many years, the American worker, whether he belonged to a unionized trade or worked in an unorganized company, had a worldwide reputation for delivering a high value for every dollar of wages, both in skill and industriousness. He still does in spite of today's "take it easy" attitude, but not nearly as much so as his father. And if the present generation of Americans does not set a better example for today's children, how much more ease-loving will the next generation be? How much more will they be prone to goldbricking and greedy chiseling?

We know that Britain is in a great deal of trouble today, and for a generation now has been dependent on our financial help to maintain even her present reduced status in the world. Foreign observers and thoughtful Britons constantly complain that Britain's worst single problem is the unwillingness of today's Englishmen to work hard or regularly or to make the adjustments necessary to cope with automation and the accelerated pace of technology. There are many psychological reasons for this, which I cannot very well go into here, but there can be no doubt that the situation exists and that it is bad. The British do not deny it, although they say, with justice, that the more malicious foreign correspondents exaggerate it. The big point is that this weariness of spirit on the part of the British populace has played a big role in continuing the inflation in Britain that in a generation has knocked the once proud pound down from an international value of $4.85 to $2.40.

It is not inconceivable that the "take it easy" attitude could do much the same thing to us over the span of the next generation. Curiously, many people seem to suffer from the delusion that work is unhealthy—"Why break your back?" "Why work yourself into an early grave?"

It is not true.

All medical authorities agree that hard work never hurt anybody. The conditions under which work is performed can be dangerous to health, and if they are, the unions and public officials should raise the devil until the conditions are changed. The mental and emotional pressures resulting from working on a job you heartily dislike or for a boss you cannot stand can be unhealthy— but not the work itself. So long as you find satisfaction in your work, the more work you do within reason, the more your health will thrive.

Your health is far more likely to suffer from the mental worries and emotional pressures of being out of work, or of deliberately loafing and consequently becoming an aimless, frustrated and totally insecure person.

This brings up the frightfully inflationary influence of the astronomical rise in the cost of medical care in our time. Better medical care is excellent for society and, in the long run, it eliminates an enormous waste of manpower. But there is a lot of cost padding in our huge national medical and hospitalization bill. On the other hand, the most expensive single aspect of the problem, the burdensome increase in the cost of the care for the mentally and emotionally ill, involves no cost padding. If anything, outlays are skimped in this most expensive of all health problems. The source of the staggering cost of mental and emotional illness is plain frustration— psychiatry lags so far behind the other branches of medicine in attaining positive results with patients. For example, most psychiatrists can do virtually nothing for a person who has a serious emotional illness except provide custodial care and stuff the patient with tranquilizing drugs. This treatment will result in intermittent apparent remissions, but almost invariably the patient relapses, and as time goes on, gets much worse and sinks into schizophrenia. Such a person can cost society a staggering sum in hospitalization care and welfare payments over a period of years, and there seems to be no way out of it. These patients cannot be left with their families; they will wreck the lives of everyone around them in short order.

The cost to society and to industry of persons who are emotionally disturbed, yet not quite ill enough to be hospitalized continuously, is probably much greater than the cost of those who are committed. And, in consequence, this is an additional inflationary force in our society.

So each citizen can help halt inflation by taking good care of his health. In that way, he not only reduces by a not insignificant amount the direct-cost burden of medical care, but he helps curb another strong inflationary influence in our economy—absenteeism from work. Every large business' accounting department is constantly appalled by the heavy cost of absenteeism caused by health problems, alcoholism, just plain laziness, and lack of incentive on the part of workers. Since hourly workers normally do not have as liberal paid-sick-leave privileges as salaried workers, it is the salaried workers who exert the worst inflationary pressures on the economy by absenteeism. Just remember that every time you take an unjustified day off with pay from your job, you and millions like you are contributing to slashing the purchasing power of your weekly paycheck.

There are several bad individual habits that have developed in modern society that exert terrific inflationary pressures. One is the "unemployment check habit." It is particularly prevalent among young people although a considerable number of older people are not above it. The unemployment check habit is even more damaging in its effects on personal character than in its inflationary influence on the economy. Persons who have the unemployment check habit make a deliberate practice of working only a part of each year, and of not taking a job seriously enough to regard it as a career. The typical young person with the unemployment check habit takes a job with the resolve to keep it just long enough to regain his eligibility for unemployment insurance. For the first few weeks on the new job he tries to fool the boss, make him think he really is interested in the job and intends to work hard. Then he starts coming in late and skipping days. When he has worked enough weeks to be eligible for unemployment insurance again, he starts really goofing off, openly shirking his duties, staying out more frequently and even being rude and disagreeable to everybody. His object obviously is to get fired or laid off. He will not quit voluntarily, because in that case he would have some difficulty collecting unemployment insurance.

If he does not get fired soon enough, the character with the unemployment check habit will fake an illness and thereby get an excuse for leaving the job that the unemployment insurance office may be forced to accept.

There are some millions of people in the United States who live this way year after year, twenty-six weeks of loafing on unemployment benefits and cadging off relatives and friends, then three to six months of working indifferently in an inferior job to build up eligibility for a new period of loafing. Meanwhile, they are losing ground steadily in the normally competitive economic arena of society and are preparing themselves for a lifetime of frustration and futility. The outright cost of this to society in extra unemployment benefits and extra overhead costs in the social services is enormous, and the inflationary influence of it on the economy is obvious. It has been wisely said, Steal my money, but don't steal my time. If you want to prevent the ravages of inflation in America, don't contract the unemployment check habit.

The "relief check habit" is akin to the unemployment check habit. We read in the newspapers of New York and other large cities of raids carried out in the apartments of women on relief, with children, in which a shamefaced able-bodied man is dragged from hiding under a bed. He is living on the woman's relief check and is either her husband or her paramour. The woman herself may have borne illegitimate children solely to make herself eligible to stay on relief rolls for a period of years and to avoid having to go to work daily.

It must be conceded that a high proportion of those who have the relief check habit are the victims of our worst social and racial discriminations, who have given up the effort to be self-sustaining out of sheer frustration, but not all. Relief rolls contain the names of some persons who could be self-sustaining, but simply do not try hard enough. In any case, our high relief costs exert another serious inflationary pressure on the economy.

A person who detests inflation must resolve to keep himself and his family off relief rolls. It should behoove our public officials to have as many persons as possible who are presently on relief rolls regain their self-respect through adequate employment.

One of the greatest of all causes of creeping inflation is crime, felony crime, petty pilferage and chiseling, malicious mischief and vandalism. The police and the casualty insurance companies can make pretty good guesses at the staggering cost to society of crime and delinquency. And, of course, our public budgets and tax bills give us some inkling of how much it costs us to operate our police, the courts and the penal system.

Our not too remote ancestors seem to us today to have had pretty barbarous ideas about enforcing justice. They maintained few prisons, just enough to keep prisoners while awaiting trial—and a third to half of those confined died before trial. Death was the penalty for half or more of all felonies. There was no right of appeal from the trial court and sentence commonly was carried out within a week of conviction.

No counsel was provided for the indigent defendant and the rules of evidence and court procedure strongly favored the prosecution, in contrast to the way criminal law is enforced today.

Barbarous as these customs were, they were at least as effective a deterrent against crime as our more humanitarian laws and customs, and they were all our ancestors could afford. It is becoming doubtful that we can afford much longer to coddle criminals and delinquents to the extent that we have in the United States since World War II. The bill for crime and delinquency is growing frightfully, and corrupt members of the legal profession, aided and abetted by misguided social workers, are constantly pressing for ever greater leniency toward criminals and delinquency and ever greater expenditure of public funds on their behalf. But the truth is that the more lenient the laws become and the more the criminals and delinquents are regarded as sick and disadvantaged persons entitled to sympathy and help instead of punishment, the more lawless American society becomes and the greater the inflationary impact of crime and widespread dishonesty on the part of the public.

The activities of organized criminals, including their undoubtedly widespread penetration into businesses that appear legitimate on the surface, is costing American society hundreds of millions of dollars yearly. But for every dollar organized crime succeeds in siphoning out of the economy, several thousand dollars are stolen by other criminals—delinquents and supposedly honest citizens with a streak of larceny.

The only way to check the inflationary impact of crime is to halt the drift to tolerance of crime and dishonesty in American society, to oppose the cynical lawyers and the misguided social workers who have a vested financial interest in maintaining a climate of undue leniency in the courts and law enforcement agencies.

Every individual who wants to halt the inflationary

impact of crime must refuse to vote for the reelection of judges who show leniency toward criminals, toss out of office lazy prosecutors who repeatedly scale down indictments and allow perpetrators of heinous crimes to plead guilty to a simple assault, vote only for candidates for the state legislature who campaign on promises to tighten the criminal laws, and thus restore the vigor of law enforcement to what it was in America before World War II. Above all, he must seek laws that will make it easy to disbar defense attorneys who try to make a circus out of the criminal courts in order to build up their personal public images. Perry Mason is wonderful on TV because his clients are always innocent, but notice that the scriptwriters are required to make Mason uncover the real murderer in every trial. The defense lawyer in real life is under no such obligation to society. He is privileged to get a thousand guilty murderers and swindlers off scot-free and is not required to do anything on behalf of society; yet he claims to be operating on behalf of society and boasts of his status as an officer of the court.

Much more important than the way an individual casts his vote—he can help reduce the inflationary impact of crime by taking an attitude toward crime based on society's interest rather than on his own selfish desire to avoid involvement. We must not be afraid to complain or prosecute. The law enforcement agencies complain constantly that business firms will not prosecute people who steal from them or give the agencies much cooperation in arresting persons for even serious disorder on their premises. The police complain that insurance companies sometimes become accomplices of criminals by buying back stolen insured property from them to reduce their losses on the claims and then withholding evidence from the police. This may not contribute directly to the inflationary cost of crime, but it certainly encourages criminals to continue to steal in the belief that they can evade prosecution by seeking the protection of the insurance companies.

Normally, though, far from being an accomplice of the criminal, the insurance company is the prime target of the thief. The bank robber waves his pistol at the cowed customers and tellers and says: "Now, take it easy everybody, and nobody gets hurt but the insurance company!" In fact, the favorite excuse of all criminals, big shots and small-timers alike, is, "We're not harming anybody but the insurance companies, and they can afford it." But it is getting to the point where soon neither the insurance companies nor society will be able to afford it.

As an insurance man, I am perforce conscious of the inflationary impact on the economy of blown-up insurance claims. Those the public is most aware of result from automobile accidents. The principal villains probably are shady lawyers who build up grossly exaggerated claims for bodily injury, where no serious injury really occurred, and shady garage operators who grossly inflate liability claims for collision damage to cars. The high cost of automobile insurance and the underwriting loss experience of the insurance companies in recent years has been a national scandal for which the public bears a large amount of responsibility.* There are also plenty of fraudulent fire insurance claims resulting from arson.

There also has grown up in our society a custom of inflating minor disability claims to such proportions that they have caused severe rises in the cost of health insurance and hospitalization—with resulting general inflationary influence on the economy.

Remember, every time a person takes the insurance company for a couple of hundred bucks too much on an automobile accident claim or lets a shady lawyer talk him into prosecuting a phony bodily injury claim and splitting the award with the lawyer, he is dealing another blow at the stability of the dollar. Don't you do it if you really want to prevent runaway inflation.

But the most important way in which an individual can help avert inflation is simply by being conscious of the inflationary peril at all times and exercising his voice strongly for restraint.

For example, a man belongs to a union. The union is presently bargaining or getting ready to bargain for a new contract. Naturally, the demands the union is making on the employers are much higher than the union officers really expect to win. The company's initial offer is much lower than management really expects to settle for ultimately. That is human nature and is common to

---

* See Arthur Milton, *Something More Can Be Done: An Involvement Booklet on Driver Safety* (New York, Timely Publications, 1965).

all bargaining. From the point of view of avoiding inflationary peril, there is always the risk that the rank and file will be led or will try to stampede their officers into demanding too much without taking account of the degree to which inflation will wipe out much of the increased package immediately. Large unions employ economists who keep them pretty well posted on this subject. The economists advise the union officers that, in a period like the present, fringe benefits are apt to be more beneficial to the union membership than large wage increases, because they partake of the nature of equity and thus cannot be immediately vitiated to a large degree by new inflation.

But the workers tend to think in terms of hourly rates and the number of hours worked. They press for shorter hours and bigger rates without understanding that creeping inflation of money can wipe out such increases within a year or two. *United States News & World Report*, in a recent article, said that inflation had cut a factory wage increase from an average of $107.53 per week in 1965 to $114.36 in 1967, to an actual drop of $1.39 per week in real terms—that is, in terms of what the weekly paycheck would buy. Inflation of the cost of living and inflation of taxes caused the decline in real wages.

Is the answer to this problem another drastic increase in factory wages? Most economists say no, that the solution lies in moderating the rise of wages and concentrating on halting the rise in the general price level, that if we try to race wages against prices, prices always will win and the workers will be on a treadmill going no-where.

So, to help halt inflation, the union member must be an influence in his union for moderation, for reasonable wage increases and more fringe benefits.

It is even more important to be inflation-conscious when a person is spending his paycheck than when he or his union are negotiating that paycheck's size with his employer. He must resist price increases he believes are unjustified by refusing to buy; resist the temptation to buy things he does not need and cannot enjoy just for show or status; and resist being extravagant about cloth-ing, entertainment, liquor and gambling. He will not have closets loaded with nearly new expensive clothes he never wears.

Above all, the conscientious citizen must strongly re-sist the demands of teenage children that they be given expensive things because other children have them, and they think they have a right to have them. They have no such right and giving in to them not only is con-tributing to the inflationary pressures of society, but has a pernicious effect on their character.

Recently, there have been signs that American con-sumers are becoming very price-conscious and are, in fact, exerting anti-inflationary pressures against business. The University of Michigan's Survey Research Center for some years has made periodic studies of the buying moods of consumers with the aim of forecasting for busi-ness the probable trends of consumer-buying during the ensuing six months. The university center has had pretty good luck with these forecasts.

The Ann Arbor forecasters have said their most recent surveys led them to believe there would be no inflationary demand for consumer goods in the immediate future. They found consumers worried about inflation and fearful of having to pay higher prices for necessities, and therefore unwilling to spend their disposable income freely.

But some other forecasters, notably some of the banking economists, felt that whatever consumer intentions were, the overall trend of the economy was very likely to be inflationary during the years immediately ahead.

A cherished belief of traditional economists is that the taxing power can be used to prevent inflation. It is a good theory and has worked in practice in the past. But under the practical conditions of modern American Government and politics, the theory that by raising taxes and hence "sopping up" the surplus buying power of the public you can exert a strong deflationary influence has been widely challenged. Congressmen, bankers, some economists and many, possibly a majority, of businessmen are quite skeptical about the notion that raising taxes really can have an effective deflationary impact unless the tax increase is accompanied by a rather drastic slash in Government expenditures.

Their reasoning is simple: Under modern conditions, Government is the biggest of all spenders in the nation, and hence raising taxes simply transfers money from the public to the Government, which is the most wasteful spender of all. If this reasoning is correct, simple logic would indicate that raising taxes can accelerate inflation instead of curbing it because, politics and human nature being what they are, the Government will simply have more money and spend it in ways that would exercise a greater inflationary effect than if the money remained in the hands of the public.

11.

LIVING WITH INFLATION

For the wealthy, living with creeping inflation has few hazards. Many rich folk manage to benefit inordinately from inflation. Their bank deposits increase, the valuations of their stocks, land, jewelry and other assets and their incomes go way up.

The kind of rich people who pride themselves on belonging to the "smart money" crowd also are good at quickly shifting large portions of their capital into the kind of assets that usually are protected even against galloping inflation.

For many years, the most popular way of hedging against inflation was to buy gold. But for Americans, this has been illegal since 1933 here at home, and since 1961 it has been unlawful for Americans to own gold anywhere in the world. Nevertheless, some Americans do buy gold bullion and store the metal illegally abroad as a hedge against galloping inflation. But since the statu-

116

tory penalty is severe in case of detection, and the cost of carrying and insuring the hoarded gold abroad may be more than the maximum rate of 3 percent a year at which the dollar has been inflated in terms of commodity prices, hoarding gold can be decidedly profitless as well as risky for Americans. The penalty can run to ten years in prison plus a $10,000 fine.

Buying shares in companies that mine gold or silver is another favorite device of the rich to enable them to sleep well in the shadow of the specter of inflation. Although, as a group, gold-mining shares do not rate particularly high with security analysts either as glamor stocks or dividend producers, they do have the merit of being very sound and any inflation that led to a new devaluation of the dollar would be bound to increase their profitability and make them go up rather sharply. Of course, in any given gold-mining stock, there is the risk that the veins of gold ore in the company's mines might suddenly peter out. Nevertheless, the stocks of some Canadian gold-mining companies have tripled in price in recent years.

Silver-mining company stocks also have become a favorite hedge against inflation for the wealthy. They have not gone up nearly so such as gold-mining shares, only about 50 percent, but the growth has been more solidly founded on a tremendous increase in the use of silver in industrial and consumer products, as well as for money in many countries.

Some rich people buy bar silver and bar platinum, which are precious metals in which Americans can speculate or invest legally. On the European markets, particularly in London, they can be bought on margin, sometimes as little as 20 percent. But that means putting up collateral for the other 80 percent and paying interest on it, as well as insurance and the initial brokerage fee. If silver and platinum keep on going up in value, all very well. However, in spite of platinum's rarity and unique qualities, anyone contemplating hoarding platinum should take into consideration that in recent years science has found excellent cheap substitutes for it. Platinum has not been important to the electric lamp industry for years, for example.

Swiss francs, which are 123 percent backed by gold in contrast with the 27 percent gold backing of the United States dollar, are another favorite inflation hedge. Their purchase is perfectly legal.

While it is illegal for Americans to buy gold bullion, it is perfectly lawful to collect gold coins having a curio value, which is about the only kind of gold coin to be had anywhere these days. So some wealthy Americans collect gold coins as an anti-inflation hedge. This costs real money. A $20 United States gold piece fetches $65 in the curio market, and an 1,800-year-old Roman coin, containing perhaps $40 worth of intrinsic gold, increased in value from around $200 in the 1940s to well over $10,000 twenty years later. Also, the dealers have a way of bidding very low on gold coins when collectors try to sell.

Everybody has read about wealthy persons collecting paintings, postage stamps, rare books and antique furniture both as a hedge against inflation and possibly to lay the foundations of a speculative fortune. Certainly the long-term price trends of good paintings and antiquities are upward, often very sharply. The difficulty for the ordinary person with a little money is that all these things are highly selective and to hedge or speculate in them successfully requires intensive study, expensive professional advice and considerable capital.

This also is true of land. The long term trend in the price of land has to be upward because, as the fellow said, "they are not making any more of it." It keeps getting scarcer. When an inflationary threat becomes acute, land prices go up more sharply than all other prices. But that does not make it easy for those without special training, expert advice and liquid capital to hedge or speculate in land. Land prices are highly selective. A corner lot may make several fortunes by appreciation and income for successive owners over a period of a few years, while a lot in the middle of the same block remains a drug on the market and a tax drain.

When land prices soar because of inflation, land income does not necessarily rise with the prices. A given parcel of land may not be suitable for any immediate use that will produce substantial income, yet the asking price for it remains very high because the owner can afford to carry it, and he knows that if somebody comes along with a use for that particular piece of land, he may need it very badly and will pay a good price.

Even if the land is being used, its income potential for the foreseeable future may be limited strictly by a long-term lease, rent controls or zoning restrictions. In consequence, inflation may have the paradoxical effect of simultaneously raising the price of a piece of land and reducing the tract's earnings in real terms.

Landlords never have been the most loved people in the world nor do they wield a large number of votes. Therefore, local governments never have been unduly concerned about landlords' welfare in times of severe inflation. The classic example of this occurred when the socialists took over the municipal government of Vienna during the severe inflation of the early 1920s. Vienna was and is a city of apartment-house dwellers. One of the more bizarre things the socialist administration did was to freeze rents at the level of the year 1917, but allow tenants to pay them in current Austrian crowns. So an apartment that had rented for the equivalent of about forty United States dollars a month in 1917 rented for less than fifty American cents in 1925.

The reason the Vienna government was so harsh on the landlords was that they had paid off all their mortgages in the grossly inflated crowns. In view of the rent freeze, the Austrian courts refused to let the city impose confiscatory taxes on the buildings, but the city could and did prevent their sale without special permission. When things got better and the landlords were able to sell the buildings or raise rents, they did not fare badly, but the moral to the story is that during an inflationary period landlords are liable to be treated roughly by public authorities. So one should be careful about trying to beat inflation by becoming a landlord.

Good common stocks, both those listed on the exchanges and those traded over the counter, such as life insurance company shares, afford one of the best hedges against inflation and one of the best ways to obtain income to meet rising prices during periods of inflation.* The stock market is very sensitive to price inflation, and frequently anticipates it, thus providing protection very quickly. The stock market, moreover, is open to investment and trading purchases by all except the poorer persons in the social scale.

In my previous books, I strongly advised all Americans who can afford to do so to put some of their savings into common stocks comparatively early in their working careers. And in a period when we are plagued by creeping inflation, I think it doubly important that prudent persons buy and hold common stocks.

But beware of becoming overextended in the stock market. Buying listed stocks on sensible margin—you cannot buy on margin in over-the-counter trading—can be a way of accumulating capital fairly rapidly, but like any method of accelerated gain, it also carries built-in risk. So long as the stocks you hold on margin keep going up, fine and dandy. If the inflationary spiral accelerates, they will go up faster and perhaps you will be able to sell some of them at a sufficient profit to pay off most of your margin debt and reduce your carrying costs—interest rates to the broker on the margin loans vary widely.

---

* See Arthur Milton, *Life Insurance Stocks; the Modern Gold Rush* (New York, Citadel Press, 1963).

But if you then get greedy and overextend yourself by purchasing an ever wider portfolio of listed securities on margin, you run a severe risk, because every inflationary spiral in the stock market must inevitably come to an end, and that end always brings a sharp drop in the prices of stocks, such as the drop that occurred in May, 1962. If the drop catches you spread too thinly in the market, you not only will lose all the paper profits you have accumulated, but your original stake as well. You can be wiped out overnight.

There are other risks in using the stock market as a hedge against inflation. Even if you do not become overextended by buying on margin, there is the risk of putting too much faith in glamor stocks that show big growth profits by advancing rapidly in price during inflationary periods, but pay rather poor dividends or no dividends. And when deflation strikes the market, these glamor stocks frequently are the hardest hit. They go down very fast, and they may remain depressed for many months, even for years. So, even though you own the stocks outright, they are not much comfort to you in the deflationary era following the inflation. And remember that deflationary waves can hit the stock market hard while the general trend of the economy is inflationary and the general price level and cost of living still are rising.

I want to emphasize again that every thinking citizen should buy good stocks, not just as a hedge against inflation, but in order to have a stake in America's growth. I think we should all be "card-carrying" capitalists.

From my own experience, I am sure that the people

who make out well in the stock market in the long run are not the speculative traders, but those who buy good-grade stocks in good solid industries and retain them for years, profiting by cash dividends, stock dividends, rights offerings and appreciation.

But the inevitable inflation accompanying the growth of the economy must be considered. I should not be astonished if, by the end of the century, the working man's salary of $7,500 today is $30,000 and the kind of automobile that is priced today at $4,000 then has a $9,000 price tag.

The best way to prepare for this era is to buy stocks sensibly. But do not get reckless in trying to use the stock market as protection against inflation. If you can use the market wisely, it is one of the best protections available.

It is hard to say to what extent the desire to hedge against inflation has figured in the great increase in stock market trading that saw daily volume on the New York and American stock exchanges rise from six million shares at the start of the 1960s to almost 20 million shares in the late 1960s. It is probable that natural growth of the economy plus plain speculative fever were greater factors than fear of inflation in the growth of the market volume.

That the growth of trading is due more to natural expansion than to any other factor is indicated by the rapid recent growth of the smaller exchanges. Smaller companies needing a liquid market for their shares have been listing in increasing numbers on the new National Stock Exchange in New York and the Midwest Exchange in Chicago as well as on the burgeoning Pacific Coast Exchange, which now has trading floors in both San Francisco and Los Angeles. It is possible to trade many of the blue chip issues on the Pacific Coast Exchange after the New York market has closed for the day.

Aside from the rich, most persons who are in business for themselves, and even salaried and hourly workers whose services are in great demand or who belong to unions with very high bargaining power, usually can manage to keep their heads above water in periods of creeping inflation. The businessman raises the prices of the goods or services he sells and the organized workers demand and get a constant stream of raises. But, as we have seen in the previous chapter, these raises in themselves accentuate the inflation, so the workers do not really get ahead; they barely keep abreast of prices at best and more commonly keep losing a little in the race with prices.

In the kind of creeping inflation that has been visited on the American economy in recent years, it is common to hear people who are living close to the edge of bankruptcy say "We'll make out all right so long as we can keep our credit good."

This is literally true, but once inflation ceases to creep and starts to walk and then to lope a little, the credit that has been so easy to get in the past suddenly dries up. The merchants, the banks and even the high-cost finance companies become increasingly reluctant to finance installment sales or to make personal loans beyond thirty to sixty days. They are fearful that if they lend dollars that are worth sixty cents in constant terms today for six months or a year, they will be repaid in dollars worth only thirty cents in constant terms. Even high financing charges that yield true annual interest rates of 20 percent or more will not come near offsetting such ruinous inflation. So credit, as we have known it in the United States since the late 1930s, simply has to vanish in the face of runaway inflation and we are right back to the days of our great-grandparents, when the only way to get things one wanted was to save the money in advance or use one's wits to make a lot of money all at once.

Sound expansion of credit based on accurate statistical information has been one of the biggest stimulants to the astonishing growth of the Western world's free-enterprise economy in the last thirty years. But everything has its price, and I sometimes fear that we pay a terrible price indeed for easy credit.

Easy credit often has a devastating effect not only on family life, but also on standards of public and private morality. The abuse of credit cards is the most obvious illustration of this. Individual stories of bizarre credit card frauds are bad enough, but suddenly we find that counterfeiting credit cards and using them to defraud the credit card companies and banks or merchants of hundreds of millions of dollars has become a lucrative racket for organized crime.

Then we learn that the Federal Reserve Board has found it necessary to rebuke many of our biggest

banks for laxity in issuing credit cards, mailing them
out indiscriminately to millions of depositors and customers without even minimal checks on their real credit
ratings. Naturally, some of the cards stray in the mails
and fall into the hands of people who proceed to forge
signatures and use them. The bankers of thirty years ago
would have regarded this as not only folly but also a
wicked betrayal of the whole philosophy of thrift and fi-
duciary responsibility to which the banking profession is
supposed to be dedicated.

The fathers of today's bankers also would be astonished at the moral tone of much of today's bank advertising, which, to put it bluntly, invites people to borrow and spend and then borrow and spend some more
and to heck with saving for a rainy day.

And how about the flippant tone of much airline and
travel advertising, which blithely tells you to travel on
credit thousands of miles "when you haven't got enough
money to go from New York to Secaucus, New Jersey"?

The whole easy-credit climate is highly inflationary,
and if you hope to live through a period of serious creeping inflation and come out of it with a whole skin, you
will have to resolutely turn your back on a lot of easy
credit in time. To live with inflation safely, you'd better
have more pay-as-you-go and much less on the pay-later
plan.

Some families will not learn how to live with inflation
for the same reason that they find it hard to get along
when conditions are normal. A writer-acquaintance told
me a story recently about an acquaintance of his in the

public relations business. His wife also was employed and they were doing quite well on joint salaries of just under $20,000 a year. Then the fellow went in business for himself and we very successful. Within a year or so, he and his wife had a joint income of nearly $50,000. But instead of saving money as they had on $20,000 a year, they were rapidly getting into debt. This state of affairs was so shocking to the PR man that he had a mild heart attack. He told my writer-friend, "My wife and I knew how to make money, but we just had never learned how to spend it sensibly, and in consequence creeping inflation was knocking us dead."

Though this is a strange story, I have seen a lot of cases pretty much like it. It is almost useless to give hard-and-fast rules for avoiding this sort of thing, because no two families have the same tastes or precisely the same financial problems. But I can give one general rule that all history and all social experience teaches us: The family should have a head who is responsible for looking after the money and budgeting the outgo, and much more often than not, the husband is the one with the knowledge and temperament to be that head. The wife may very well be thrifty, but the husband is much more apt to have the proper training and temperament to make sound long-range financial decisions.

Reckless spending or even ordinary foolish spending wrecks more marriages than infidelity or all the other cardinal sins. It causes constant bickering and even cruel bitterness between husband and wife right in front of the children, destroys the children's respect for the parents and shatters family unity, making home life hellishly uncomfortable and humiliating.

Yet many families never quite manage to grasp the simple fact that the secret of living happily within the family income is to budget the income and stick to the budget, doing without luxuries the budget won't permit. People get into extravagant habits and cannot break them though they are absurd on the face of it.

Some people are unhappy unless they dine out in an expensive restaurant four or five nights a week, while other couples think one fancy dinner a month away from home is plenty. Some families are content to invest in a good television set and get most of their entertainment on it at an annual cost of a little over $100. Others spend $1,000 or more on theater and stadium tickets. When creeping inflation starts to pinch, the families that do not break these extravagant habits in a hurry get in real trouble.

What causes otherwise sensible people to fritter away their money on these extravagances anyway? I suppose most psychologists would say it is escapism—a vain seeking for realization of romantic dreams that are based on silly illusions. "Stuff and nonsense! Get down to earth," our forebears would have snorted, "or you will end up in the poorhouse!" And not too many years ago that's exactly what would have happened to the foolish spenders.

Curiously, however, in countries that have been afflicted in recent years by severe inflation, the ingenuity of the businessman and the banker have found ways to keep business going without the kind of credit we are used to. One method widely practiced is to peg all credit deals to gold or a foreign hard currency. If a Brazilian borrows a sum of cruzeiros or purchases goods on credit, he may have to promise to repay not at the price on the day of sale, but at a price to be determined on the day the note falls due by the current value of the cruzeiro in relation to gold or dollars. The Brazilian might sign a contract to buy a television receiver priced at 325 cruzeiros on credit for a year, but with the final price pegged to the dollar. He discovers within three months that the base price has risen to 400 cruzeiros with interest and finance fees rising accordingly. If the buyer's income has gone up as the cruzeiro's value fell, he is not hurt, but if he is a workingman, chances are it has not gone up fast enough.

But such ingenuity never is sufficient to prevent runaway inflation from pressing cruelly on millions of persons who simply cannot find ways to increase their income. What of the elderly and the infirm, the very young and inexperienced and the millions of others who simply lack the mental agility or psychological adaptability to cope with the squeeze between rising prices and a paycheck that just won't stretch? What happens to these persons? They suffer and they "innovate."

To sociologists and psychiatrists, the term innovate does not just mean doing something new. It has a sinister meaning. The social innovator is the person who is driven, by his or her inability to succeed within the framework of society's accepted rules of conduct, to start making his own rules of conduct, rules by which he can be successful without regard to the rights or interests of others.

The businessman driven to such innovation starts cutting corners, engaging in unfair competition and chiseling on customers and suppliers and lenders. Little by little, sometimes rather quickly, he is driven by desperation, accompanied perhaps by an expanding ego, into outright fraud and swindling.

The workingman who becomes desperate and cannot find relief either by means of additional work or public or private charity may be driven to innovate, too. His first innovative impulse may very possibly be to steal from his employer, then to steal from others and to get into the business of selling stolen goods as a sideline to his regular job. Or he may get into check forgery or some other unlawful racket, even holdups.

Women, too, may be driven by desperation to innovation, to stealing and swindling. But many weak women who become desperate as the result of an inflationary squeeze turn to prostitution. Weak young women prostitute themselves. Weak older women and not a few men turn to pandering.

Now we come to what, in the long run, is the most subtle and difficult aspect of living with inflation: the individual's obligation as a citizen to exercise a restraining influence on Government and public officials.

I said at the end of the previous chapter that the Government is the most wasteful spender of all, and ergo the biggest contributor to inflationary pressures. It follows that, as inflation gets more serious, every one of us should use his ballot to demand curbs on wasteful spending and fiscal irresponsibility on the part of the Government.

The sad fact is that nearly all of us are doing the exact opposite. We are busy seeking Government subsidies, Government contracts or other public outlays on behalf of our own businesses or special interests while we give lip service to the idea of overall cost-cutting by the federal, state and local governments.

Of course, this problem of the citizen's duty to insist on fiscal responsibility and sound business practices by national and local government should be obvious at all times. But it is most obvious in periods of serious creeping inflation, periods like the present. Now is the time to put the brakes on spending in Washington.

But the record shows that the American people usually have not put the brakes on Government spending until it was too late. A national economy caught up in serious inflation is like a big truck running downhill on a winding road. If the driver does not use his brakes promptly, disaster is inevitable.

But, as a rule, the American people do not start putting on the brakes until the nation's economy has reached the bottom of the inflationary hill, deflation has set in and the economy starts the painful climb back up hill to what we think of as normal. When we start yelling to the Government to cut expenses, often it has already been forced to do so by running out of money. That is what happened in the 1930s. The national and local gov-

ernments were almost broke and unable to pay for necessary services, much less spend money on needed recovery measures, yet everybody was yelling illogically for
more expense-cutting.

The time to cut expenses is while the economy is still
expanding and, even then, what is important is to eliminate waste and reckless spending by Government rather
than simply to set an arbitrary ceiling on expenditures.

For the private citizen or the corporation, a balanced
budget is always essential, but economists cannot agree
on any formula that will enable the United States Federal Government to balance its budget annually at the
present time and still cope with our vast needs for expensive domestic reforms, plus our global foreign aid and
military and diplomatic commitments. The best that most
economists can envision is that, by continually expanding our total output of goods and services, we can keep
our annual deficits under a reasonable measure of control until some of our more expensive burdens can be
relinquished.

The debilitating effect on public and private morality
of wasteful spending by national and local government
and the growing attitude of people in all walks of life
and in all conditions that they should look to Government for financing and guidance throughout their whole
lives is enormous.

Even worse is the growing philosophy that anybody
who tries to be industrious and make his own way in
the world is a sap, because by exercising a little ingenuity and telling a few lies, he could live off public hand-

outs indefinitely. Businessmen who advocate enormous programs of public expenditures that will make profits for them although they serve little or no real useful purpose are harming the fabric of American society just as much.

But it does not stop there. Our newspapers are filled with stories about businessmen and other people who are not satisfied with inflated profits to be made out of boon-doggling government contracts. They also steal money from the Government, millions of dollars at a time, by gross swindles and plain burglary.

Of course, the most wasteful of all Government spending is on the armed forces and the war in Vietnam. Even if you agree, which I do not, with the Congressional majority that appears to think the war in Vietnam is a Holy Crusade on behalf of mankind, you still have to hold your nose when you read about the stench of corruption surrounding the war effort—billions of dollars in cash and war matériel paid for by American taxpayers being siphoned into the hands of black-marketers and corrupt military and civil officials in both Vietnam and our own country.

The war in Vietnam also has many Americans confused about its moral and political meaning. It gets increasingly difficult to say for whom or for what we are fighting there, and the cost, in human misery, in American lives, in money, and in the global prestige of the United States is growing at an appalling rate.

All this indicates that living with inflation and doing something sensible about it makes the sternest demands on us as citizens. It asks us, indeed, to stand up and be counted, to be counted on the side of common sense and sober decency instead of on the side of more inflationary gain for ourselves as individuals.

12.

THE ANSWER
IS WORK

In the last analysis, there is only one answer to the problem of halting inflation when it really gets out of control. The answer is *work*.

The only lasting counterbalance to inflation is increased production. Drastic deflation is like a massive dose of an antibiotic drug, but just as antibiotic drugs will not do anything against a virus infection, only against bacteria, so drastic deflation does not get at the root cause of inflationary forces in the economy. It only deals with the symptoms.

The root cause of inflation is more likely to be under-production and underconsumption than financial malaise. All the things we talked about as causes of inflation in Chapter 10 are less important than the basic matter of continuing to expand the output of goods and services. When the output of goods and services goes up faster than the supply of money, that has to bring prices down or put the brake on their advance so that they go up only in proportion to improved real values—better quality, greater usefulness or longer life, for example.

Nowadays we have a barometer of production called the gross national product, the GNP. The Federal Government keeps track of the GNP's rise and fall and regularly makes predictions as to how much it will rise or fall in the months ahead. So do economists who work for the larger banks and those who are on the staffs of important universities, research foundations and business trade associations.

Exactly how the GNP is arrived at is not so important. Suffice it to say that it represents the total annual output of goods and services within the United States of the American people. Goods produced by American companies in foreign countries are part of the GNP of those countries.

It is important, though, that we recognize a considerable difference between reports and forecasts of the current GNP of the United States and statistics of the GNP of years in the past. The GNP for past years is expressed invariably in what the economists call "constant dollars"; that is, the figures have been readjusted to reflect the price level of a given year or an average price level for a period of years. In recent years, the average price level for the years 1957–59 has been used to represent constant dollars and when you read statistics about the GNP for years since 1959, but before the current year, all the prices of goods and services involved have been readjusted, downward in most cases, to the 1957–59 prices.

In that way, the rise of the GNP can be measured in what is called "real terms"; that is, in the actual output in tons of merchandise or amounts and hours of service even if these are all expressed in dollars. By reducing the GNP to these constant dollars, the economists are able to establish with rough accuracy that the economy of the country has grown in a given year at 2.5 or 3.5 or 4 percent a year.

On the other hand, the current GNP and forecasts for the GNP in the months immediately ahead must be expressed in current dollars, which admittedly are inflated by comparison with the constant 1957–59 dollar. This is so because the economists cannot determine in advance just how much price inflation will occur in the months ahead.

So we may read in the newspapers various forecasts by Government agencies and different groups of economists that the GNP will rise by 6, 7 or 8 percent in the next six months or the next year. That sounds like a big leap forward in comparison with the actual rate of gain in the GNP in recent years. But then we read a few paragraphs farther on and learn that the economists, even those who are forecasting an 8 percent gain in the GNP, warn that they expect almost half of the gain to be pure price inflation, and that after other adjustments, they doubt if the growth of the GNP in real terms will exceed 2.5 percent.

It is pretty obvious that if production of physical goods is going up only 2.5 percent while the prices of all those goods go up 7 or 8 percent, that means inflation is going to accelerate.

But there are other straws in the wind to look for. Does the actual state of business indicate that all this price inflation will take place for sure? Perhaps not. For example, suppose we look at the increase in the GNP for the year that is just closed and see if we can find out how well business and consumers absorbed the increased output and the inflated prices. One thing to look for is the figure for inventory accumulation.

Thus, we may discover that while the GNP rose by $16 billion—in current not constant dollars—in the most recent quarter, economists already have discovered that the accumulated inventories of goods by manufacturers, distributors and retailers during that quarter increased by $4.8 billion. Therefore, the net increase in goods and services immediately absorbed by consumers was only $11.2 billion.

Now this $4.8 billion increase in inventory obviously is a potentially deflationary influence. Unless something happens to make business firms and consumers more eager to buy these inventoried goods, they will exercise a braking effect on rising prices.

Another thing to look for in trying to determine how inflationary the actual economy is must be the rate of personal savings, because this indicates how much ordinary folk are resisting the temptation to rush out and buy things. Thus, we may discover from government figures that the rate of personal savings in this final quarter of the year just closed rose to 7.5 percent of net income from 6 percent a year earlier, according to the Department of Commerce. These savings are expressed in current not constant dollars, but it is not necessary to reduce the savings figure to constant dollars to see that people actually were saving considerably more of their income than they were a year earlier, because the higher percentage obviously is applicable to a higher base. This increase has to be a deflationary influence.

There are two more very important questions we need answers to when we start looking critically at the rate of growth of the GNP. The first is, What proportion of our total industrial capacity is being utilized to produce the gain?

The economists tell us that if the utilization of existing plant capacity is extremely high, up around 90 percent, then the economy is probably becoming "overheated" and we are in the middle of a fairly serious creeping inflation. This is true because production cannot be increased much more in order to build up inventories and put a brake on rising prices. That is partly because a great deal of the 10 percent of our factory, mill, mine and transport capacity that still is not being used is obsolete and so high-cost that if we are forced to use it, we will perforce be pushing costs up still more and adding to the inflationary pressures.

But if utilization of plant capacity is below 85 percent, there still are reasonably modern idle factories and mines that can be brought back into production without running up costs too high. Of course, idle production facilities do not necessarily mean plants and mines that are closed; they may be running, but not full blast.

And as we have remarked in previous chapters, if the utilization of labor is approaching "full employment," which in our times means that the number of people not employed is below about 3.6 percent of the working force, this can be another indication that the economy is becoming overheated; however, most economists and all sociologists believe that the American economy can be restructured to utilize a much higher proportion of the working force, and that ultimately the maximum rate of unemployment that should be tolerated can be reduced to at least 2 percent. But it would be quite naïve to suggest that there is any immediate hope of such a happy condition.

The other big question we need to know the answer to is how the actual rate of the GNP compares with the optimum potential rate. The potential rate does not mean a full-capacity rate. As veteran economist Stuart Chase explains in his book *Money to Grow On*, the American economy operated at full capacity during World War II when every plant in the country ran full blast around the clock with a reckless disregard for the way machinery was being worn out.*

Some economists call the optimum potential rate of

---

* Stuart Chase, *Money to Grow On* (New York, Harper & Row, 1964).

growth of the economy the "short fall" rate—just short
of full potential at a normal eight-hour day for most industries and around-the-clock operation only for those
industries whose processes or public service requirements
make that imperative.

Chase and economists who agree with him argue that
the economic potential grows with the increase in population and the improvement in technology and that in
our era, the short fall or optimum potential growth rate
of the United States economy should be at least 4 percent a year when reduced to constant dollars.

There is widespread agreement among economists,
from the more conservative to the more radical, that the
rate of growth of our GNP has lagged consistently behind this growth potential ever since the Korean War.

And it is the failure of our economy to grow as fast as
it should that explains most of our creeping inflation and
much, but not all, of our continued inability to crack the
problems of hard-core unemployment.

Chase, who has been a leader of the liberal economists ever since the 1930s, describes the problem this
way:

> It is not so much a matter of pushing up a statistical
> gross national product as it is of shifting the use of na-
> tional resources to give the United States first a bal-
> anced structure of private and public investment, and
> second, full employment, based on full education; with
> potential output achieved, the economic growth rate
> might well be calibrated with the growth of popula-
> tion. Only the Federal government can engineer this

shift. . . . The Federal government makes the overall
fiscal and monetary decisions; private business does
most of the work. . . . A modern economy can afford
anything it can produce.†

The metaphysicians and some psychologists who agree
with them say man can produce anything he can imagine and that imagination is the ultimate dynamic of the
universe. If both the metaphysicians and economists who
agree with Chase happen to be right, then, by simple
logic, we can afford anything we can imagine if we will
work hard enough to make it happen.

The proposition that work is the only real answer to
the problem of inflation is just as important to the individual as to society. Of course, a man can practice drastic deflation by cutting his spending in order to cope
with high prices; he will have to do so. This will have a
very salutary effect on inflationary abuses if many millions of persons start practicing thrift simultaneously. But
to get at the root of personal inflationary peril each individual will have to increase his income, and one way or
another, that means working harder.

Fortunately, during periods of inflation extra work
usually is not hard to come by. At the very time when
the unemployables cannot find work, good workers are
besieged with offers of chances to moonlight on part-
time jobs.

If you take a moonlighting job in a worthwhile productive enterprise, one that produces useful goods or

---

† *Ibid.*

genuinely useful services, you may be making a very substantial contribution thereby to halting inflation. If you increase your production and practice sensible thrift at the same time you are making two contributions to halting inflation.

Not only are moonlighting jobs rather plentiful in times of creeping inflation, but one of the causes of creeping inflation is the shortage of skilled manpower—and womanpower—with a serious attitude toward work. We have such a shortage of manpower and executive talent in the United States at present, in nearly all business and professional categories. Historically, there has never been a period when there were so many opportunities for young people and persons in the prime of life to pursue a prosperous and satisfying career.

Personally, I think one of the best ways to improve your chances of earning more or producing more is to keep yourself physically fit by taking plenty of exercise. If you feel logy most of the time, you will not have the energy to work harder or longer hours. Getting plenty of exercise will make you feel like getting up and going after things during working hours. Walking, riding a bicycle, golf, tennis, handball, swimming, sailing and gardening are all good ways to get exercise. The best ways to exercise, to my thinking, are the cheapest ways. If you spend a lot of money on your exercise hobby, you may be tempted to overdo it in order to justify the expense, and overdoing it can lead to heart disease or other disorders.

A number of our Presidents have been noted for

keeping physically fit. Harry Truman could walk the legs off even the youngest White House correspondents. Teddy Roosevelt was such a bug on physical fitness that he took judo lessons while he was in the White House and he once issued an order forbidding military and Naval officers on duty in Washington to ride in automobiles or trolley cars. He said they should either walk or ride horseback! This seemed a little bizarre in 1902, and Teddy soon was talked into revoking the order. But he instituted an annual fitness test that required every Army officer either to ride a horse a hundred miles in three days or walk fifty miles in the same time. Unfortunately, that didn't last too long either.

One of the best ways to improve your personal efficiency and capacity for work is to give up smoking. Smoking not only is expensive, but it certainly cannot be healthy. If you must smoke, medical authorities say it is probably better to smoke during the relaxed hours than during the hours of comparative tension in the office. Personally, I think smoking is bad anytime, day or night. Not alone should one consider such fatal disabilities as lung cancer, but one must also think about the effect smoking has on your vital organs and your entire system.

For many years, Europeans have scoffed at Americans, claiming we eat and drink and loaf ourselves into early graves. And they are right about it.

Overeating and overdrinking not only are extravagant, but they are simply terrible for your health. As a life insurance man I have to keep up with the medical evidence on this subject, and it is overwhelming; we do overeat insanely, and we drink too much from the standpoint of taking on calories, although such international statistics as exist on the subject indicate that we have about the least alcoholism of any advanced nation. But we need not be too complacent about that—the statistics are not terribly comprehensive.

So the chances are that you and your family can safely cut down on your daily calorie intake, help fight inflation and improve your health simultaneously. Instead of the old adage "An apple a day keeps the doctor away," let's change it to "Fewer calories can mean deflation for your future medical bills and healthier, happier living."

Don't hesitate to be thrifty on the specious plea that if you cut your expenditures you would be hurting the economy. You have no obligation to help business or industry make inflationary profits at the expense of society in general and of yourself in particular. There inevitably will come a time when penuriousness on your part would be damaging to the economy and society, but that time is not while inflation is rife. Rather, that time will come, as it did in the early 1930s, after drastic deflation is already well under way.

How shall you be thrifty in a way to help halt inflation? I have already described the most important ways to be thrifty in Chapter 10, but there are others.

The first things for a sensible person to economize on when he decides to curb inflation by means of thrift are gambling, liquor, and entertainment. These are our worst extravagances. Next, I would suggest that you downgrade your purchases generally. For nearly twenty years, Americans have been "trading up" on everything from underwear to automobiles, high-fidelity phonographs to expensive homes. Much, probably most, of this trading up represents the acquisition of genuine lasting superior values. But a lot of it is mere status-symbol buying, deliberate extravagance.

Try getting along on fewer and cheaper clothes. Try riding the bus to work instead of driving and paying a parking lot fee. Resist the temptation to buy gadgets and novelties. Be satisfied with the music on a moderately priced FM radio instead of twelve-dollar albums on a thousand-dollar high-fidelity set.

Above all, buy less on credit. When you have to buy on credit, shop around and get the best credit terms. In spite of all the books and magazine and newspaper articles that have appeared on the subject, millions of Americans still seem unable to grasp the simple fact that a stated 5 percent interest rate on an installment purchase contract runs to a true annual interest rate of almost twice that.

But don't economize on your family's basic food supply or on health and insurance protection.

I started to write, do not economize on the food bill, then I realized that you can economize on the food bill, and in all probability enjoy a better and more balanced diet as a result. How? By buying more bulk foods and taking the time to do more old-fashioned kitchen work.

The big cause of higher food costs in America today

is in the packaging. Costs of food at the farm are not notably inflated. The billions of dollars our government pays out annually in farm subsidies keep the prices of basic food, except meats, down.

By purchasing bulk foods as much as you can, you can eliminate some of the high cost of packaging and factory processing costs. The packaging people and the food manufacturers won't like this, but you may like it tremendously, and there is no doubt that if a lot of people did the same, it would have a considerable deflationary influence.

Still another way to give inflation a sock in the jaw is to engage in barter whenever you get a chance. Accept due bills instead of cash for services rendered if you can use them. Restaurants and resort hotels in this country issue millions of dollars worth of due bills every year, and there are agencies in New York, Chicago and one or two other large cities where you can trade a due bill you do not particularly want to use for one offering something more to your liking.

Accept and give payment in barter, either in goods or labor. When money does not change hands, there can be no inflationary impact, and quite often a barter deal is tax free, whereas the same transaction would be subject to both sales tax and income tax if carried out in cash.

By now, perhaps it has occurred to you that it takes work to practice thrift. So, at both ends of the scale, the real way to halt inflation is for all of us to work at it.